MARY TAYLOR
FRIEND OF CHARLOTTE BRONTË

MARY TAYLOR

Friend of Charlotte Brontë

Letters from
New Zealand and Elsewhere

Edited, with Narrative, Notes,
and Appendices, by
JOAN STEVENS

1972
Auckland University Press
Oxford University Press

FIRST PUBLISHED 1972

PRINTED IN NEW ZEALAND
IN 11 ON 12 POINT
INTERTYPE TIMES ROMAN
BY JOHN McINDOE LTD
DUNEDIN

Preface

Mary Taylor has always been of interest to readers of the life or the novels of Charlotte Brontë, for obvious reasons. This volume, however, was originally planned not as an addition to Brontë lore, but as a book of New Zealand concern, since Mary's experience in this country as a middle-class spinster settler was unusual, and her report upon it articulate, lively, and shrewd.

It soon became obvious that a purely local emphasis would be insufficient; Mary's life was all of a piece, and her colonial experience has to be seen in its European context. As the investigation of her background proceeded, it illuminated not only her letters from New Zealand, but aspects of the Brontë story, solving some of its minor problems by the way (the identity of the 'Château de Koekelberg', for instance). It has also illuminated the quality of life in what has been called 'the *Shirley* Country', that complex group of manufacturing families in the West Riding of Yorkshire among whom Mary Taylor was born.

The Gomersal-Birstall area into which Charlotte Brontë's friendship with the Taylors and the Nusseys so fruitfully took her was a 'far more populous and stirring neighbourhood' than the moorland parish of Haworth (WS no. 483). A network of cousinship in all its degrees bound its families together generation after generation, in a community of interests largely related to the manufacture of woollen goods, while occupations in land, law, finance, the Church, and even Dissent, completed the circle. Comprehending it through Mary's correspondence, one begins to appreciate what *outsiders* the Brontës were in Yorkshire, among Nusseys, Carrs, Battyes, Cockills, Greenwoods, Walkers, Dixons, Taylors, etc. Their racial and intellectual isolation is as striking as their physical moorland solitude.

The presentation of this story has not been easy, because of its double interest. Brontë enthusiasts may not need all the Yorkshire explanations, while what is obvious to a Wellingtonian may require a footnote outside these islands. In view of substantial errors in New Zealand detail in previous accounts, I have erred on the side of fullness of explanation. There is no attempt at a comprehensive bibliography, but a list is appended of MSS, articles and books to which reference is made in the editorial text.

I have many people and institutions to thank for help. These libraries gave me access to their MSS, and where necessary permission to print: Henry W. and Albert A. Berg Collection of the New York Public Library, Astor, Lenox and Tilden Foundations; British Museum; Brontë Parsonage Museum, Haworth; Brotherton Library, University of Leeds; Fitzwilliam Museum (Allbutt Bequest), Cambridge; Henry E. Huntington Library, San Marino, California; Leeds City Museum; Manchester University Library; Miriam Lutcher Stark Library, University of Texas; Pierpont Morgan Library, New York.

I am indebted to Mr A. D. Taylor for permission to publish the letters of Mary and Martha Taylor; to Miss M. Rathbone for permission to quote from the letters of the Dixon family; to the Alexander Turnbull Library, Wellington, for the photographs in Plates 1 - 5, and to A. De Boeck, Brussels, for the illustration in Plate 6.

My debt to librarians, colleagues and many willing informants is indeed heavy, though all cannot be named. I wish however to thank in particular Miss Rona Clark of Victoria University Library; the staff of the Brontë Parsonage

Museum, Haworth, and the Alexander Turnbull Library, Wellington; Dr M. G. Christian, Mrs Lock (Winifred Gérin), Mrs Trench, Mr Walter Cunliffe, Mr Hellewell, and Captain C. H. H. Owen. Mr John T. M. Nussey gave me invaluable assistance with family records in Yorkshire. Miss Andrée Art, of the Université Libre de Bruxelles, pursued for me the search for the Château de Koekelberg. In New Zealand, I have had great help from members of the Taylor family, Mrs Mildred Dalrymple, Mrs Deborah Spencer, and Mr F. M. Gardner.

Note on the Text

Mary Taylor's letters have been transcribed from the MSS or photostats in all except six instances (nos. 1, 3, 30, 31, Appendices B and C) where the originals have not been traced. In their presentation, some modifications have been made for the reader's comfort. The ampersand, '&', is rendered as 'and', Dr, Mr, etc have been normalized, full stops have been supplied wherever it is certain that Mary intended one. Errors in completing brackets or quotation marks have been silently corrected. Abbreviations have been expanded within square brackets wherever the full word is not obvious. Letters or words inadvertently omitted have been conjecturally supplied when possible, as have omissions due to blots or mutilation. Mary's own deletions have been ignored, except where they seem of some significance, when a footnote is given.

Mary's spelling of 'Bronte', without the diaresis, has been corrected throughout, but her spelling 'Ann', for Anne Brontë, is not touched. Other spelling errors are left unaltered, but are checked in a footnote.

Insertions are indicated by solidi / /, and lacunae by angle brackets ⟨··⟩ . The addressee, date, WS number, and location of the MS are given at the head of each letter.

Quotations from Charlotte Brontë's letters have as far as possible been checked in the original MSS, but the text given is that of Wise and Symington unless there is significant variation. Quotations from her novels are from the Haworth edition, edited by C. K. Shorter, 1899-1900. Quotations from Mrs Gaskell's *Life of Charlotte Brontë* are from the same edition, 1900.

These abbreviations are used in the notes and references:

A.T.L.	Alexander Turnbull Library, Wellington.
BST	*Brontë Society Transactions.*
Burke *LG*	John Burke, *A Genealogical and Heraldic History of the Landed Gentry* (various dates).
CB	Charlotte Brontë.
DNZB	*Dictionary of New Zealand Biography,* ed. G. H. Scholefield. 2 vols. Wellington, 1940.
EN	Ellen Nussey.
MT	Mary Taylor.
SBC	C. K. Shorter, *Charlotte Brontë and her Circle.* London, 1896.
SLL	C. K. Shorter, ed. *The Brontës: Life and Letters.* 2 vols. London, 1908.
WS	Thomas James Wise and John Alexander Symington, ed. *The Brontës: their Lives, Friendships and Correspondence.* 4 vols. Oxford, 1932.

Contents

Illustrations

List of Taylor Letters

Page

PART ONE

Yorkshire

The survival of the letters of Mary Taylor is wholly due to her association with Charlotte Brontë and Ellen Nussey, for her own family kept none of the correspondence that passed during her long years away. Charlotte may have saved some letters, we do not know, but Ellen, that pious and devoted magpie, hoarded everything that she could lay hands on, both letters to herself, and letters which she acquired as the last recipient in a circle of friends who passed the news around. Mary Taylor's letters in this way became included in the Brontë corpus, and passed safely with it into the strongrooms of Brontë collectors.

Mary's place in literary history, too, insignificant though it may be, is due to the Brontës. Though she herself published articles and a novel, it is for her presence in the novels of her friend that she is best remembered, for Charlotte gave the Taylors literary immortality in *Shirley* and *The Professor*. Inevitably, then, this account of Mary Taylor must begin in Yorkshire, with Taylors, Brontës and Nusseys, who met for the first time at Miss Wooler's school at Roe Head, Mirfield Moor, in 1831.

Mary Taylor, born 26 February 1817, was the fourth child of Joshua Taylor of the Red House, Gomersal, and at the date of meeting Charlotte Brontë was just fourteen, while Ellen Nussey was two months younger, and Charlotte almost fifteen. The Taylors were a complex family unit centred in the West Riding, mostly engaged in woollen manufacture and its associated trades, and banking. There were Taylor cousins, and Dixon cousins, and Mossman cousins, all located in Leeds or Bradford or thereabouts, and all from the same 'peculiar, racy, vigorous' stock (*Shirley,* chapter 9).

Gomersal is a village lying to the east of Cleckheaton between Bradford and Huddersfield, on rising ground above the River Spen (see Plate 1). Perhaps the best way to evoke it as it was in the 1830s is to quote Charlotte Brontë's description in chapter 2 of *The Professor:*

> The autumn sun, rising over the — — shire hills, disclosed a pleasant country; woods brown and mellow varied the fields from which the harvest had been lately carried; a river, gliding between the woods, caught on its surface the somewhat cold gleam of the October sun and sky; at frequent intervals along the banks of the river, tall cylindrical chimneys, almost like slender round towers, indicated the factories which the trees half concealed; here and there mansions, similar to Crimsworth Hall, occupied agreeable sites on the hillside; the country wore, on the whole, a cheerful, active, fertile look. Steam, trade, machinery had long banished from it all romance and seclusion. At a distance of five miles, a valley opening between the low hills, held in its cups the great town of X— —. A dense, permanent vapour brooded over this locality.

The 'great town' is Huddersfield, the smoke of which was visible from Roe Head school. In this district, close now to the highroad from Gomersal to Bradford, and about a mile from Birstall and its Church at the bottom of the hill, stands the Red House, built in 1660 by William Taylor. It has just been acquired by the Spenborough Council both for its own sake and to house items of local history. The Red House is so named from its warm red bricks, which distinguish it from its neighbours in an area characterized by grey stone. It is a pleasant, low-set, two-storied house, with gables and wide lawns, and with auxiliary buildings at the rear which in Mary's time included not only the usual stables, barn, coach house, etc, but a strong little stone building used until the crash of 1825 for her father's banking business. Inside, the Red House is still gracious; a Dutch-tiled entrance hall is surrounded by a first-floor gallery, off which open the bedrooms and a passage leading to the servant's room. The main rooms below are well proportioned and substantial; the stained glass windows which in Mary's day screened the parlour from the eyes of back-door callers have been removed, and were presented by the family to the Brontë Parsonage Museum at Haworth.[1]

William Taylor the builder of the Red House was followed by John I, born in 1650, and he by Joshua I, born in 1700 (see Table A). Joshua's son John II (1736-1805) built mills in 1780, a mile or so up the River Spen in the 1200 acre Hunsworth estate, and did very well in his special line of manufacturing army cloth, which he exported to France and Italy. He married Anna Waring of Idle (1739-1817) and fathered a family of eight children, of whom five appear by name in Mary's records. Because of their business interests in Europe, the Taylor family in these years became much more cosmopolitan than their Yorkshire neighbours. It will be noticed in Table A that one son, James, married a French girl.

John Taylor II's eldest son, Joshua II (1766-1840) was Mary's father; he is the 'Hunsden Yorke Hunsden' of *The Professor,* and the 'Hiram Yorke' of *Shirley,* 'a French-speaking Yorkshire gentleman', whose 'matted hall' of entrance was 'lined almost to the ceiling with pictures', and whose 'large parlour' also exhibited his taste, 'the taste . . . of a travelled man, a scholar, and a gentleman' (*Shirley,* chapters 3 and 4). Charlotte added, however, that 'the harshness of the north was seen in his features, as it was heard in his voice', and that he had 'an indocile, a scornful,

[1] See Edward Taylor's note on this in Stevens, 'Sidelights on *Shirley', BST* 1969, p. 308.

and a sarcastic face; the face of a man difficult to lead, and impossible to drive'. His wife, née Anne Tickell, does not seem to have earned her children's affection. Charlotte disliked her, and put her into the novel as an 'ungenial matron', large, grave, burdened with a 'voluntary, exemplary cloud' of gloom, and characterized by a 'funereal dreariness of tone' such as befitted the voice of an experienced 'kill-joy' (*Shirley*, chapters 9, 23). On her husband's death in 1840, all but her eldest son promptly left her, and even he broke away for good in 1845 (WS no. 219).

As 'Hunsden Yorke Hunsden', Joshua Taylor II is a bachelor, but in *Shirley* the more extensive portrait shows him with his wife and children. His eldest son, Joshua Taylor III (1812-80) appears in the novel as 'Matthew Yorke', the tyrant of the family, 'sceptic and scoffer', with a spirit compounded of 'flame and shadow'. 'Mrs Yorke' is afraid of the boy's temper, and always conciliates him. Joshua III is the brother whom Mary never mentions in her letters, nor does he appear in Charlotte's correspondence. The next two brothers, however, John IV (1813-1901) and Joseph (1816? -57), entered a great deal into their sister's life. John, the 'Mark Yorke' of the novel, was a 'calm boy with a cutting tongue'; he emigrated to New Zealand in 1875 or 1876 and died unmarried. Joseph, who as 'Martin Yorke' is given an attractive rôle, was undoubtedly for a time Charlotte's hero. His affairs are constantly discussed in her letters. After alarming his friends and relations in the 1840s by the number and variety of his flirtations (WS nos. 150, 151, 197, 215, 219, 243, 265, etc), he finally settled on Amelia Ringrose, whom he married in 1850. He died at the early age of forty-one.[2]

Next among the children of Joshua Taylor II was Mary, pictured as 'Rose Yorke', followed by Martha (1819-1842), who is 'Jessy', and lastly William Waring (1819?-1903), who does not appear in the novel. He emigrated to New Zealand just after his father's death and married here, where numerous descendants remain today. His life is discussed in the

[2] See Edward Taylor's note, *BST* p. 309: 'Joe, was a clever practical and theoretical chemist, and practically CB's hero.'

Introduction to Part III.

Two more generations of Yorkshire Taylors must be noted. Mary's eldest brother Joshua III, who married in the Moravian Church at Gomersal in 1838, provided her with four nephews, of whom the eldest, Joshua IV, had in his turn two sons, Joshua James and Thomas Sigston Taylor. To these two great-nephews Mary left her little property on her death in 1893, with the exception of an annuity to her brother John, who had not made a success of life.

Charlotte Brontë's portrait in *Shirley* of her two friends Mary and Martha Taylor, as 'Rose' and 'Jessy' needs to be given in greater detail. She introduces them in formal character-pieces in chapter 9, 'Briarmains', where the Red House and its inmates are described.

> The two next are girls, Rose and Jessy; they are both now at their father's knee, they seldom go near their mother, except when obliged to do so. Rose, the elder, is twelve years old; she is like her father—the most like him of the whole group—but it is a granite head copied in ivory; all is softened in colour and line. Yorke himself has a harsh face; his daughter's is not harsh, neither is it quite pretty; it is simple—childlike in feature; the round cheeks bloom; as to the grey eyes, they are otherwise than childlike—a serious soul lights them —a young soul yet, but it will mature, if the body lives; and neither father nor mother have a spirit to compare with it. Partaking of the essence of each, it will one day be better than either—stronger, much purer, more aspiring. Rose is a still, sometimes a stubborn girl now: her mother wants to make of her such a woman as she is herself—a woman of dark and dreary duties—and Rose has a mind full-set, thick-sown with the germs of ideas her mother never knew. It is agony to her often to have these ideas trampled on and repressed. She has never rebelled yet; but if hard driven, she will rebel one day, and then it will be once for all. Rose loves her father: her father does not rule her with a rod of iron; he is good to her. He sometimes fears she will not live,

so bright are the sparks of intelligence, which, at moments, flash from her glance and gleam in her language. This idea makes him often sadly tender to her.

He has no idea that little Jessy will die young, she is so gay and chattering, arch — original even now: passionate when provoked, but most affectionate if caressed; by turns gentle and rattling; exacting yet generous; fearless—of her mother, for instance, whose irrationally hard and strict rule she has often defied—yet reliant on any who will help her. Jessy, with her little piquant face, engaging prattle, and winning ways, is made to be a pet; and her father's pet she accordingly is. It is odd that the doll should resemble her mother feature by feature, as Rose resembles her father, and yet the physiognomy—how different!

The account of the family is then summed up in these words:

Take Mr Yorke's family in the aggregate, there is as much mental power in those six young heads, as much originality, as much activity and vigour of brain, as— divided amongst half-a-dozen commonplace broods— would give to each rather more than an average amount of sense and capacity. Mr Yorke knows this, and is proud of his race. Yorkshire has such families here and there amongst her hills and wolds—peculiar, racy, vigorous; of good blood and strong brain; turbulent somewhat in the pride of their strength, and intractable in the force of their native powers; wanting polish, wanting consideration, wanting docility, but sound, spirited, and true-bred as the eagle on the cliff or the steed in the steppe.

This portrait of her home and family seemed to Mary to be true enough. On reading the novel in New Zealand in 1850 (Letter 21), she wrote: 'You make us all talk as I think we shd have done if we'd ventured to speak at all— What a little lump of perfection you've made me! There is a strange feeling in reading it of hearing us all talking. I have not seen the matted hall and painted parlour windows so plain these 5 years. But my Father is not like. He hates well enough and perhaps loves too but he is not honest enough.'

Later, Mary gave some glimpses of her home life to Mrs Gaskell. Recalling Charlotte's visits to the Red House in their girlhood, she wrote 'We used to be furious politicians, as one could hardly help being in 1832.' Mary was 'of the furious Radical party,' and the two friends 'used to dispute about politics and religion. She, a Tory and clergyman's daughter, was always in a minority of one in our house of violent Dissent and Radicalism' (Appendix B, first letter, extracts 4 and 8). At the Taylor's house, Mary added, 'we had a rage for practicality, and laughed all poetry to scorn. Neither she nor we had any idea but that our opinions were the opinions of all the *sensible* people in the world, and we used to astonish each other at every sentence' (Appendix B, second letter, extract 1).

Another sidelight on these portraits in *Shirley* is given in the annotations to the novel made by Edward Taylor, 'Hiram Yorke's' grandson (*BST*, 1969, pp. 304-17). He wrote: 'Yorke was the late Mr Joshua Taylor, his character is well, but much overdrawn'. And again, 'Yorke's house is well drawn, . . . The interior details are very correct as when I lived in it.' Two of his comments in particular illuminate Charlotte's words 'intractable', 'wanting docility', 'turbulent'; etc. First, Taylor is discussing this episode:

Mr Yorke is addressing Moore, 'who had thrown himself into an old-fashioned chair by the fireside—"Move it, Robert! Get up, my lad! That place is mine. Take the sofa, or three other chairs, if you will, but not this; it belangs to me, and nob'dy else."

' "Why are you so particular to that chair, Mr Yorke?" asked Moore, lazily vacating the place in obedience to orders.

' "My father war afore me, and that's all t'answer I sall gie thee" '.

On this, Edward the grandson wrote, 'Chair still exists and much the same idea in its present owner Yorke's eldest son . . . . This chair was known as John Wesley's Chair, as he alone was allowed to use it beside the head of the house when he was present.' (*BST*, 1969, p. 306).

On the description of Yorke in chapter 4—his 'inelegant, unclassic, unaristocratic mould of visage', his bigotry, pride, and impatience of control,—Edward Taylor noted that 'most of the characteristics are fairly present in the two following generations.' In particular, he commented on the words 'Revolt was in his blood: he could not bear control; his father, his grandfather before him, could not bear it, and his children after him never could', by adding 'nor his grandchildren.' One begins to see why Mary Taylor had the independence and courage to do so many unusual, even outrageous things. Her strength of character was, it seems, inherited.

As *Shirley* proceeds, Charlotte Brontë develops her portrait of Rose Yorke-Mary Taylor a little further. A revealing passage occurs in the conversation between Caroline Helstone (herself partly drawn from Ellen Nussey) and the Yorke womenfolk in Chapter 23. Caroline asks Rose her opinion of Mrs Radcliffe's *The Italian*. Rose replies, 'It makes me long to travel . . . . I mean to make a way to do so, if one is not made for me. I cannot live always in Briarfield. The whole world is not very large compared with creation: I must see the outside of our own round planet at least . . . . I am resolved that my life shall be a life . . . [not] a long slow death like yours in Briarfield Rectory.' Later, Rose amplifies this: 'Better to try all things and find all empty, than to try nothing and leave your life a blank. To do this is to commit the sin of him who buried his talent in a napkin—despicable sluggard!'

This remark prompts Mrs Yorke to insist that a woman's proper place is the home, whereupon Rose puts up a spirited defence of her views. 'Mother, the Lord who gave each of us our talents will come home some day, and will demand from all an account. The tea-pot, the old stocking-foot, the linen rag, the willow-pattern tureen, will yield up their barren deposit in many a house: suffer your daughters, at least, to put their money to the exchangers, that they may be enabled at the Master's coming to pay Him His own with usury.'

This belief, that women had a duty as well as a right to earn an independent living, is one which Mary held with passionate conviction, as her life and her writings show.

To return for a moment to others of the Taylor family who will appear in Mary's correspondence. In the generation of her father four more persons must be noted. (See Tables A and B).

They are Mary's aunt Mary (1767-1850), who married a Leeds merchant, Chapman; her aunt Sarah (1769-1851); her uncle William (1777-1837), who married Margaret Mossman; and her aunt Laetitia (1780-1842), who married Abraham Dixon.

Laetitia Dixon's children included George (later M.P. for Birmingham), Thomas, and Mary, the last in particular being of importance, since she befriended Charlotte Brontë in Brussels. The children of William Taylor and Margaret Mossman were William Henry (1828-99) and Ellen (1826-51), both of whom joined Mary and Waring Taylor in New Zealand. Ellen became Mary's partner in the shopkeeping enterprise at Wellington.

Oddly enough, to complete the circle of relations whose Continental travels created the links between Brussels and Yorkshire which transformed Charlotte Brontë's life, the Mossman family had later connections with her school, the Heger Pensionnat. Ellen Taylor's cousin, William Mossman, married a girl who had studied there, and in due course sent his own two daughters there also. (See Table B, and Stevens, *BST*, 1971).

It was in January, 1831, that Mary Taylor first met Charlotte Brontë and Ellen Nussey at Miss Wooler's school, Roe Head, Mirfield. In 1855 Mrs Gaskell, hearing of their long association, wrote out to Mary in Wellington to ask for help with material for the *Life*. The result was two admirable letters, full and perceptive, which Mrs Gaskell relied upon heavily and quoted extensively (Gaskell, *Letters* nos. 256,

314a, 348). Mary's narrative of Roe Head life has been a quarry for biographers ever since. (See Appendix B). It was supplemented later by Ellen Nussey, who supplied also her impressions of Mary. These latter were published by C. K. Shorter in 1896 in his *Charlotte Brontë and Her Circle*. Ellen wrote (pp. 234-6):

She was pretty, and very childish-looking, dressed in a red-coloured frock with short sleeves and low neck, as then worn by young girls. Miss Wooler in later years used to say that when Mary went to her as a pupil she thought her too pretty to live. She was not talkative at school, but industrious, and always ready with lessons. She was always at the top in class lessons, with Charlotte Brontë and the writer; seldom a change was made, and then only with the three—one move. Charlotte and she were great friends for a time, but there was no withdrawing from me on either side, and Charlotte never quite knew how an estrangement arose with Mary, but it lasted a long time. Then a time came that both Charlotte and Mary were so proficient in schoolroom attainments there was no more for them to learn, and Miss Wooler set them Blair's *Belles Lettres* to commit to memory. We all laughed at their studies. Charlotte persevered, but Mary took her own line, flatly refused, and accepted the penalty of disobedience, going supperless to bed for about a month before she left school. When it was moonlight, we always found her engaged in drawing on the chest of drawers, which stood in the bay window, quite happy and cheerful. Her rebellion was never outspoken. She was always quiet in demeanour. Her sister Martha, on the contrary, spoke out vigorously, daring Miss Wooler, so much, face to face, that she sometimes received a box on the ear, which hardly any saint could have withheld. Then Martha would expatiate on the danger of boxing ears, quoting a reverend brother of Miss Wooler's. Among her school companions, Martha was called "Miss Boisterous," but was always a favourite, so piquant and fascinating were her ways. She was not in the least pretty, but something much better, full of change and variety, rudely outspoken, lively, and original, producing laughter with her own good-humour and affection. She was her father's pet child. He delighted in hearing her sing, telling her to go to the piano, with his affectionate "Patty lass."

Mary never had the impromptu vivacity of her sister, but was lively in games that engaged her mind. Her music was very correct, but entirely cultivated by practice and perseverance. Anything underhand was detestable to both Mary and Martha; they had no mean pride towards others, but accepted the incidents of life with imperturbable good-sense and insight. They were not dressed as well as other pupils, for economy at that time was the rule of their household. The girls had to stitch all over their new gloves before wearing them, by order of their mother, to make them wear longer. Their dark blue cloth coats were worn when *too short,* and black beaver bonnets quite plainly trimmed, with the ease and contentment of a fashionable costume. Mr. Taylor was a banker as well as a monopolist of army cloth manufacture in the district. He lost money, and gave up banking. He set his mind on paying all creditors, and effected this during his lifetime as far as possible, willing that his sons were to do the remainder,[3] which two of his sons carried out, as was understood, during their lifetime—Mark and Martin of *Shirley.*

In view of Ellen's comment that Mary was 'pretty', it is to be regretted that no portrait exists earlier than the one in the Brontë Parsonage Museum, which shows the oblong 'granite head' of a formidable old lady in a cap. But Charlotte wrote in *Shirley* (chapter 23) about Mary's 'grey, remarkable eyes'.

[3] Joshua Taylor II's will makes no mention of this. Edward Taylor, son of Joshua III, writes that 'Joshua Taylor . . . carried out the payment of his father's debts, who was brought down by the failure of a cousin—Dixon of Birmingham' (Stevens, 'Sidelights on *Shirley*', *BST* 1969, p. 306). Joshua Taylor III is, of course, the 'Matthew Yorke' of *Shirley.*

Ellen Nussey (1817-97), the second of the trio, was also from a well-established Yorkshire family (see Table C). She was the thirteenth and last child of John Nussey of Birstall Smithies, one of a large clan of cloth manufacturers, whose members included some famous Londoners, the Royal Apothecaries Richard Walker senior, Ellen's great-uncle; Richard Walker junior, her father's cousin; Joseph Nussey her uncle; and John Nussey, her eldest brother.[4]

At the date when Ellen was sent to Roe Head, she was living with her widowed mother at Rydings, the home of her old bachelor uncle Richard Nussey. Rydings was a battlemented Manor House, which it is conjectured may be partly recalled in Charlotte Brontë's Thornfield Hall in *Jane Eyre* (Nussey, in *BST*, 1968). In 1837 Mrs Nussey moved to a smaller house, Brookroyd, not far away, where also of course Charlotte often stayed. The Nusseys at Rydings and the Taylors at the Red House were only about a mile apart, and Charlotte came to know all three houses well. Her impression of the Taylors has already been given, shining through her novels. Here is her view of Ellen, recorded in 1850:

> When I first saw Ellen I did not care for her—we were schoolfellows—in the course of time we learnt each others faults and good points—we were contrasts—still we suited—affection was first a germ, then a sapling— then a strong tree: now—no new friend, however lofty or profound in intellect . . . could be to me what Ellen is, yet she is no more than a conscientious, observant, calm, well-bred Yorkshire girl (WS no. 512).

Mary Taylor's letters strengthen the impression one derives from Charlotte's references that Ellen was softer than her two dominant friends. Unlike them, she neither left home nor made any attempt to earn her living, in spite of their persuasions. Certainly an ageing mother was a tie, and there were other responsibilities; the long illness of her sister Sarah, who died in 1843, and the mental decline of her

[4] See John T. M. Nussey, in *Medical History,* January 1970.

brother George are both noted in Mary Taylor's letters. She did not marry, though she seems to have been on the brink of it at least in 1840, when Charlotte wrote her several letters of advice. In one letter that November, Charlotte based her suggestions upon what she and Ellen had jointly observed of an affair between Mary Taylor and Branwell Brontë. (WS no. 106, but see pp. 16-17 following.) And if Mary was attracted to Branwell, the circle may be said to be completed by the marriage proposal made to Charlotte by Ellen's brother Henry (Gérin, pp. 124-9). Undoubtedly Charlotte remembered the Rev. Henry Nussey when she drew St John Rivers in *Jane Eyre*.

In these ways Charlotte Brontë's friendship with Mary and Ellen gave her an insight into the closely-knit community of the Gomersal-Birstall area, which we may legitimately term 'the *Shirley* Country'. The tangle of relationships, generation after generation, that was woven to and fro between these clans can be appreciated only by a study of family trees. The Brontës were outsiders, from another race, but Ellen and Mary were native to the land and its folk. Mary's many references to their common friends reveal what an intricate network there was.[5]

Also at Roe Head was young Martha Taylor, Mary's sister, lively and rather spoilt. One of Martha's letters from school survives, and gives a happy picture of the life, even if she was unlikely to win Miss Wooler's coveted 'neatness prize'; it is given in Appendix C.

Something must be said here of Miss Wooler and her sisters. Margaret Wooler was the eldest of a large family, also native to the district. Born in 1792, she was just on forty when Mary, Ellen, and Charlotte entered her school in 1831. Ellen described her as 'like a lady abbess', while Charlotte put her into *Shirley* as the aloof but lovable Mrs Pryor. Aiding her at Roe Head were her sisters Catherine (b. 1796), Susan (b. 1800) who had just married the Rev. E. N. Carter, curate of nearby Mirfield Parish Church, Marianne (b. 1802), and Eliza (b. 1808).

[5] See Genealogical Tables A to E.

Charlotte left the school in June 1832, and spent the next three years at home in Haworth. In July 1835 she returned to Roe Head as Miss Wooler's assistant, taking Emily with her as a pupil, the fees to be defrayed by Charlotte's services. But Emily could not endure the life and Anne soon took her place. Mary Taylor disapproved of Charlotte's giving 'so much for so little money', but the arrangement lasted until 1837. In that year Miss Wooler moved to Dewsbury Moor, where in the damper climate Anne fell ill. Panic-stricken, Charlotte blamed Miss Wooler for neglect, and Anne was withdrawn. She herself stayed on until May 1838. The resulting coolness between Charlotte and her old headmistress lasted some years, but friendship was renewed with later understanding. Not long afterwards, Miss Wooler handed the school over to her sister Eliza, and later offered the reversion of it to Charlotte, who however by that time was organized for Brussels. After withdrawing from her school, Miss Wooler lived with her sister Mrs Carter at the Vicarage, Heckmondwike, not far from Ellen Nussey at Birstall; there are constant references to her in Mary's letters home.

After they left school in 1832, the three friends never lost touch with one another; Charlotte stayed at Rydings for the first time in September 1832, escorted there by Branwell, and again in February 1835. (WS, vol. I, pp. 105-6, 126). Ellen visited Haworth in the summer of 1833 (WS, vol. 1, pp. 110-16). Since Charlotte was the isolated one, her letters to Ellen—which alone survive—often contain messages for Mary. 'Your account of Miss Martha Taylor's fit of good behaviour amused me exceedingly, I only hope it may be permanent', she wrote on 5 September 1832, adding a request to 'Polly'—her nickname for Mary—for a letter to show that she was 'yet in the land of the living' (*BST* 1964, pp. 46-9).

In 1833, it was 'Poll' Taylor's turn to demand a letter (Charlotte called her friend both 'Poll' and 'Pag'). She was in 'high dudgeon', wrote Charlotte in June, 'at my inattention in not promptly answering her last epistle' (WS no. 27). Thus although Mary's own letters of this time do not survive, we have news of her in Charlotte's. With Mary she exchanged letters upon literary, political, and intellectual matters, while Ellen preferred the personal tone (WS no. 35). The Brontë-Taylor exchanges were not calm and placid like the Nussey correspondence, as may be seen from Charlotte's remarks to Ellen in September 1836 (WS no. 52): 'Last Saturday afternoon being in one of my sentimental humours I sat down and wrote to you such a note as I ought to have written to none but M. Taylor who is nearly as mad as myself; today when I glanced it over it occurred to me that Ellen's calm eye would look at this with scorn.'

That summer of 1836, in May and June, Charlotte had stayed with the Taylors at the Red House, one of several such visits in these years (see extract 8 of the first letter and extract 1 of the second letter in Appendix B). Stimulating, exhausting visits they were, but 'one of the most rousing pleasures I have ever known', as she later remembered (WS no. 74). Mary at this time was often unwell, and in August 1837 went with Martha for three weeks holiday in Wales. Upon their return in October, Charlotte was able to report to Ellen, who was in Somerset, that Mary's trouble was not the 'disease in the lungs' which the Brontës so understandably dreaded, but 'a disordered stomach' (WS no. 65). In June 1838, Martha and Mary stayed for a few days at Haworth, and Charlotte again reported to Ellen (WS no. 68).

Mary Taylor is far from well. I have watched her narrowly during her visit to us. Her lively spirits and bright colour might delude you into a belief that all was well, but she breathes short, has a pain in her chest, and frequent flushings of fever. I cannot tell you what agony these symptoms give me . . . . Martha is now very well; she has kept in a constant flow of good-humour during her stay here, and has consequently been very fascinating . . . . They are making such a noise about me I cannot write any more. Mary is playing on the piano; Martha is chattering as fast as her little tongue can run; and Branwell is standing before her, laughing at her vivacity.

The Taylor girls stayed at Haworth again in February-March 1839. Early in the next year, 1840, Ellen spent three weeks with Charlotte, when Mr Brontë's new curate William Weightman was the focus of flirtation. Martha Taylor, who got wind of some aspect of the fun from Ellen on her return to Brookroyd, was devoured with curiosity (WS no. 91). By May 1840, Charlotte's letters were full of good advice about a Mr Vincent who was in the offing as Ellen's suitor. In June, Charlotte spent a few days at Gomersal with Mary; this was followed by Mary's visit to Haworth, when she also sampled the delights of Mr Weightman's company (WS nos. 97, 98). 'Mary Taylor's visit has been a very pleasant one to us', Charlotte wrote, 'and I believe to herself also. She and Mr. Weightman have had several games at chess which generally terminated in a species of mock hostility'.

Branwell was at home that June of 1840. But by November, whatever had developed between Branwell and Mary had been checked. This is clear from an unusually full letter which Charlotte sent to Ellen in connection with the same Mr Vincent about whom she had given advice in May. Feeling rightly that Ellen's affair was 'high and important', Charlotte delivered 'a discourse and a piece of advice' on the proper behaviour for a young woman at such a crisis. Ellen must not indulge in the 'romantic folly' of waiting for 'une grande passion'. To fall in love, and show it, *before* marriage, is disastrous (a view which Charlotte had obviously abandoned before she wrote her novels). To reinforce her precepts, Charlotte offered her friend an example with which they were both familiar, the experience of Mary Taylor. Ellen kept this letter safely, but in view of its contents scored out several passages, including two long paragraphs relating one to herself and one to Mary.

R. B. Haselden (*Bib. Soc Trans.* 1935) penetrated the secret of the passage about Ellen, from which it is clear that Mary also had been consulted about Ellen's dilemma. But the passage relating to Mary is irrecoverable except for a few words, as indicated here. The text is from the MS. in the Henry E. Huntington Library; WS give it as letter number 106, but with no indication that a passage about Mary has been omitted. In addition, the letter is misdescribed in **M. G.** Christian's *Census*.

(Postmark 'No. 21' i.e, November.
The year is 1840.)

. . . .

    Did I not once tell you of an instance of a Relative of mine who cared for a young lady till he began to suspect that she cared more for him and then instantly conceived a sort of contempt for her—? You know to what I allude—never as you value your ears mention the circumstance—but I have two studies—*you* are my study for the success the credit, and the respectability of a quiet, tranquil character. Mary is my study—for the contempt, the remorse—the misconstruction which follow ['s' *del*] the developement of feelings in themselves noble, warm—generous—devoted and profound—but which being too freely revealed—too frankly bestowed —are not estimated at their real value. God bless her— I never hope to see in this world a character more truly noble—she would *die* willingly for one she loved—her intellect and her attainments are of the very highest standard.

    [Here 6 lines of the MS. have been scored out. Words that can be read include: 'your destiny has . . . *thought her* . . . doubts . . . the fact that she wd . . . really marry . . . merely brought to a pitch of great intensity seldom equalled . . . . I did not value her the less for it because I understand.' The readable text then resumes with 'yet I doubt,' etc.]

yet I doubt whether Mary will ever marry.

From the phrasing of 'Did I not once tell you', it may be inferred that the episode was well in the past. We know no more than this. Perhaps this affair is one reason why Mary kept only one of Charlotte's letters to her, the impersonal one of September 1848, and why on her return to Yorkshire after Charlotte's death she would never discuss her friendship with the Brontës.

At the end of this same year of 1840, life changed dramatically for the Taylors; their father died at Christmas, and
the family at the Red House broke up. Joshua Taylor II left
his property, still encumbered with debts resulting from the
failure of his bank in 1825, to his wife Anne, with his sons
Joshua III and John IV as executors. Joshua III took over
the house, and lived there with his difficult mother until
1845, when her 'unhappy disposition' led them to separate
(WS no. 219). John and Joseph moved to a cottage at the
back of the family's Hunsworth Mill, about a mile away,
which Charlotte came to know well, and put into *Shirley* as
'Hollows Mill'. Martha was to be sent almost at once to a
finishing school in France. As for Mary, Charlotte was sure
that she would take a more adventurous course. Writing to
Ellen on 3 January 1841, she said (WS no. 107):

> What will be the consequence of his [Joshua Taylor's]
> death is another question; for my own part, I look for-
> ward to a dissolution and dispersion of the family, per-
> haps not immediately but in the course of a year or
> two. It is true, causes may arise to keep them together
> awhile longer, but they are restless, active spirits, and
> will not be restrained always. Mary alone has more
> energy and power in her nature than any ten men you
> can pick out in the united parishes of Birstall and
> Gomersal. It is vain to limit a character like hers within
> ordinary boundaries—she will overstep them. I am
> morally certain Mary will establish her own landmarks,
> so will the rest of them.

Within a month or so, Mary's unorthodoxy became apparent. She proposed to emigrate to New Zealand, with her
youngest brother William Waring. Had she done so at this
date she would have been an Early Settler indeed, for the
first body of Wellington's citizens had landed here only the
year before, in January 1840. On 1 April 1841, Charlotte,
now governessing for Mrs White of Upperwood House,
Rawdon, wrote to Ellen to arrange a day's outing, and
added: 'Now mind Nell—I am not coming to Birstall with

the idea of dissuading Mary Taylor from going to ⟨··⟩ New Zealand—I've said everything I mean to say on that subject —and she has a perfect right to decide for herself' (WS no. 111; text from the MS. at Huntington Library, which has a passage of two or three words obliterated before 'New Zealand').

The next day Charlotte explained the matter more fully to her sister Emily, in a letter which gives us valuable insights into Mary's motives (WS no. 112).

Matters are progressing very strangely at Gomersal. Mary Taylor and Waring have come to a singular determination, but I almost think under the peculiar circumstances a defensible one, though it sounds outrageously odd at first. They are going to emigrate—to quit the country altogether. Their destination unless they change is Port Nicholson, in the northern island of New Zealand!!! Mary has made up her mind she can not and will not be a governess, a teacher, a milliner, a bonnetmaker nor housemaid. She sees no means of obtaining employment she would like in England, so she is leaving it. I counselled her to go to France likewise and stay there a year before she decided on this strange unlikely-sounding plan of going to New Zealand, but she is quite resolved. I cannot sufficiently comprehend what her views and those of her brothers may be on the subject, or what is the extent of their information regarding Port Nicholson, to say whether this is rational enterprise or absolute madness.

What the upheaval was in the Taylor household which is indicated by Charlotte's 'very strangely' and 'peculiar circumstances' is not known. In view of the absence in Mary's letters of any references to her brother Joshua, perhaps the trouble lay there. As for the choice of New Zealand, a little more explanation needs to be offered.

The establishment of colonies in new lands as a solution to social and economic problems in Britain was a major issue in the first half of the nineteenth century. Emigration seemed to many thoughtful men and women to be a 'rational enterprise' which offered them their only hope of health and prosperity. America, Canada, South Africa, Australia, attracted adventurers and settlers in increasing numbers. It was left however to an erratic genius, Edward Gibbon Wakefield, in conjunction with a group of Radical thinkers called the Colonial Reformers, to formulate a theory of systematic colonization and to organize its practical application. The first settlement launched under this theory was that in South Australia in the mid 1830s.

There had been glances cast at New Zealand earlier than this. A commercial company was promoted in 1825, which even managed to send off an expedition, but the venture failed. It is of interest however to our concerns here to note that among its Directors was John Dixon, banker, of Birmingham, after whom Wellington's Dixon Street was later to be named (Irvine-Smith, p. 61). It is probable that he was one of the Dixon clan to whom Mary Taylor was related.

Renewed activity on New Zealand matters led in 1837 to the forming of the New Zealand Association, shaped according to Wakefield's theories, which sought to have a Royal Charter and broad powers of government in the setting up of a colony. It met strong opposition at once from the powerful missionary influence in the Colonial Office, which feared for the rights of the Maori people should further encroachments be made. The Association was blocked, and reformed in consequence as the New Zealand Company, an independent commercial enterprise on the joint-stock principle. This was set up in August 1838, and among its Directors in early years were Sir William Hutt, M.P. for Hull, Edward Gibbon Wakefield himself, and Sir William Molesworth, Radical M.P. for Leeds. Among those working for its interests was also Thomas Attwood, Birmingham banker and Radical M.P., whose daughter Angela had married Edward Gibbon Wakefield's brother Daniel in 1835.

This new New Zealand Company began at once to raise funds; investment was solicited, land orders were sold, and a campaign for settlers was mounted widely, particularly in the south and west of England, in Yorkshire, and in Scotland. By the middle of 1839 there was sufficient in hand —some £400,000 in shares of £100 each—to make it possible to finance an expedition for the purchase and survey of suitable land. Increasing opposition within the Colonial Office led the Directors, rightly, to suspect further official interference; to forestall it they hastily sent off their Principal Agent, Colonel William Wakefield (another brother) in the *Tory* in May 1839, with the survey ship *Cuba* following in July. Wakefield arrived in August, and proceeded at once, without adequate investigation of Maori title, to negotiate the sale of large areas of land at Port Nicholson, Nelson, Wanganui, and Taranaki. The improper haste of these proceedings created grave difficulties in the early years of these settlements.

Meanwhile the Company in Britain collected its settlers, held a ballot in London to decide the order in which holders of land orders might select their slices when the survey should be completed, and chartered its ships for the transport of the adventurers. Among the Company shareholders were, of course, not only those who intended to set out in person, but also the speculators who intended to stay at home. Sir William Molesworth, his mother, and his sister held shares, for instance, while his brother Francis emigrated to Port Nicholson and himself worked on his land in the Hutt Valley. Many men of wealth and position who made the voyage stood as sponsors to working class settlers from their own district, so that little 'county pockets' developed at first in the new land, reflected in such names as New Plymouth, or Cornish Row, the name of some flax huts on the banks of the Hutt River in 1840. A useful discussion of early proceedings will be found in W.H. Oliver's *The Story of New Zealand*, 1960.

It is in this context that we must consider the decision of William Waring Taylor and his sister Mary to emigrate to 'Port Nicholson, in the northern island of New Zealand.' When Mary finally came, in 1845, she paid her own passage, but Waring came at a reduced fare as an 'intermediate passenger', though he was not of course sponsored as a working man. There were Yorkshiremen already in Wellington at the time that the Taylors were making these decisions, a group having sailed on the *Oriental* in September 1839. In particular, three brothers from the '*Shirley* Country', James, Joseph, and Edward Greenwood, were early arrivals. James left in September 1839 on the *Duke of Roxburgh,* Joseph in the *Lady Nugent* in January 1841, so that there were established links between the West Riding and Wellington. These Greenwood men were distant relations of the Greenwoods of Knowle Mills, Keighley, who in various ways come into the Brontë story (see Gérin, pp. 142-51). One member of this great family group had married a Heaton of Ponden Hall, another a Swaine of Gomersal. The Taylor menfolk may well, then, have had contacts in New Zealand, so that Mary's idea was not 'absolute madness'.

By May 1841, Martha had gone off to her school, but in Brussels, not in France. In June, Charlotte had an offer of a teaching post in Ireland. She passed it on to Mary, who refused it: 'I offered the Irish concern to Mary Taylor but she is so circumstanced that she cannot accept it—her brothers—like George [Ellen's brother]—have a feeling of pride that revolts at the thought of their Sister "going out". I hardly knew that it was such a degradation till lately' (WS no. 115).

By August 1841, both Martha and Mary were away from their native Yorkshire, enjoying the 'great advantages' of foreign travel. Mary's letters about the experience fired Charlotte to 'wish for wings', and led directly to the most dramatic and stimulating period of her life, the years at the Heger Pensionnat at Brussels. Alone at Upperwood House one Saturday evening that August, Charlotte confided in Ellen (WS no. 119):

Martha Taylor it appears is in the way of enjoying great advantages—so is Mary—for you will be surprised to hear that she is returning immediately to the Continent with her brother John—not however to stay there but to take a month's tour and recreation—I am glad it has been so arranged—it seemed hard that Martha should be preferred so far before her elder Sister—I had a long letter from Mary and a packet—containing a present of a very handsome black silk scarf and a pair of beautiful kid gloves bought at Brussels—of course I was in one sense pleased with the gift—pleased that they should think of me—so far off—amidst the excitement of one of the most splendid capitals of Europe—and yet it felt irksome to accept it—I should think Mary and Martha have not more than sufficient pocket-money to supply themselves I wish they had testified their regard by a less expensive token.

Mary's letter spoke of some of the pictures and cathedrals she had seen—pictures the most exquisite—and cathedrals the most venerable—I hardly know what swelled to my throat as I read her letter—such a vehement impatience of restraint and steady work. Such a strong wish for wings—wings such as wealth can furnish—such an urgent thirst to see—to know—to learn —something internal seemed to expand boldly for a minute. I was tantalized with the consciousness of faculties unexercised—then all collapsed and I despaired.

In September, Martha sent a note to Ellen about her 'month's tour' with Mary and John.

LETTER 1

Martha Taylor to Ellen Nussey, 9 September 1841; text from WS no. 120.

Brussels 9 September 1841

My Dear Ellen,

I received your letter from Mary, and you say I am to write tho' I have nothing to say. My sister will tell you all about me, for she has more time to write than I have.

Whilst Mary and John have been with me, we have been to Liége and Spa where we staid eight days. I found my little knowledge of French very useful in our travels. I am

going to begin working again very hard, now that John and
Mary are going away. I intend beginning German directly.
I would write some more but this pen of Mary's won't write,
you must scold her for it and tell her to write you a long
account of my proceedings. You must write to me sometimes. George Dixon is coming here the last week in September, and you must send a letter for me to Mary to be for-
warded by him.[1] Good-bye. May you be happy.

                         Martha Taylor.

    Prior to this, the Brontë girls had been considering setting
up a school of their own, and Charlotte had seriously
thought of accepting Miss Wooler's offer of her school at
Dewsbury Moor. But now, as Charlotte put it, 'a fire was
kindled', and Mary Taylor 'cast oil on the flames—encour-
aged me and in her own strong energetic language heartened
me on—I longed to go to Brussels' (WS no. 123). So she
asked her aunt Miss Branwell for help in financing a period
for herself and Emily at a school abroad, where they could
perfect their languages. She wrote on 29 September (WS
no. 121):

Martha Taylor is now staying in Brussels, at a first-rate
establishment there. I should not think of going to the
Château de Kockleberg, where she is resident, as the
terms are much too high; but if I wrote to her, she, with
the assistance of Mrs Jenkins, the wife of the British
Consul, [Rev. Evan Jenkins, British Chaplain] would be
able to secure me a cheap and decent residence and respectable protection. I should have the opportunity of
seeing her frequently, she would make me acquainted
with the city; and, with the assistance of her cousins
[the Dixons] I should probably in time be introduced to
connections far more improving, polished, and cultivated, than any I have yet known.

[1] George Dixon, Martha's cousin, who will take over to Brussels
the letter which Ellen will send to his sister, Mary Dixon, for
forwarding. Cross-Channel postage was expensive. For the Dixon
and Taylor relationships, see Tables A and B.

Aunt Branwell agreed to help. Letters were written to Belgium at once, but Mary warned Charlotte that they could 'hardly expect to get off before January'.

Meanwhile, Mary's youngest brother Waring took the New Zealand plunge without her. He sailed in the *Martha Ridgway*, which carried a contingent of settlers for the New Zealand Company's new colony at Nelson, among them several sponsored from Yorkshire. Leaving on 7 November 1841, Waring arrived in Wellington in April 1842 (Stevens, *BST*, 1969).

In the latter part of 1841, Mary seems to have been back at Hunsworth, to judge by Charlotte's letter of 10 December. By that date she had heard of a 'less expensive establishment' than the 'Château de Kockleberg'. Help had been sought, as planned, through the Jenkins family. Ellen was acquainted with the Rev. David Jenkins, perpetual Vicar of Pudsey, brother of the British Chaplain at Brussels, whose son was the curate at Batley, near Birstall. (See Martha's remark on 4 April 1842, in Letter 2). Charlotte may have described the latter as an 'unclerical little Welsh pony' but he was useful (WS no. 161).

There was a temporary check, when Mrs Jenkins reported so unfavourably on the schools in Brussels that the plan was switched to Lille, a step which Charlotte regretted since she would not have the company of the Taylors. 'Mary has been indefatigably kind in providing me with information' she told Ellen on 20 January 1842, '—she has grudged no labour and scarcely any expenses to that end—Mary's price is above rubies—I have in fact two friends you and her staunch and true—in whose faith and sincerity I have as strong a belief as I have in the bible—I have bothered you both—' (WS no. 129).

But, as Winifred Gérin put it (p. 180), 'at the eleventh hour, however, Mrs Jenkins wrote to recommend yet another school with which she put Charlotte in immediate touch. It was the Pensionnat Heger'. And so, on 8 February 1842, with Mary and Joseph Taylor as their couriers, Charlotte, Emily and Mr Brontë crossed the English Channel to the Brave New World ahead.

PART TWO

Brussels and Germany

The morning after their arrival, Mary Taylor joined her sister at the Koekelberg school, always referred to among the girls as the 'Château'. It was conducted by Madame Goussaert, wife of Norbert Goussaert, 'rentier'. She was English born, being the daughter of Robert and Ann Phelps of Stoke Damerel, Devon, where she was christened Catherine in October 1794. She was therefore forty-seven at the date of Mary Taylor's arrival at her Pensionnat des Dames in the suburb of Koekelberg, near the Chaussée de Jette, outside the gates to the north-west of Brussels. Details of the school and its site, hitherto an unsolved problem for Brontë biographers, will be found in Appendix D. See Plate 6 and the map on page 172.

Abraham Dixon, Mary's uncle, was living in the city, in the Rue de la Régence, where members of his family often visited him. Mary, his only surviving daughter, was constantly there, while his fourteen year old nephew William Henry Taylor worked with him in some kind of apprenticeship. Also in Brussels was Dixon's fifth son, Thomas, studying engineering and taking German lessons from King Leopold's librarian. George, the fourth son, who worked for a Birmingham firm, travelled to and fro, as did John and Joseph Taylor. Uncle Abraham Dixon had plans, too, for

'Aunts Chapman and Sarah', his wife's sisters, whom he
wished to bring over to Ostend to live. In addition, he
cherished a benevolent scheme for Ellen Taylor, Henry's
sister, that she should join the Brontës at the Heger Pensionnat. Like so many of his plans, this came to nothing, though
it was still being canvassed as late as 1848 (WS no. 379).
Obviously the Dixon-Taylor group in Brussels was complex
and united; indeed, Brussels at this time seems almost to
have become a Riding of Yorkshire.

At Easter 1842, shortly after their arrival, Charlotte and
Emily went out to the 'Château de Koekelberg' to spend the
day; one result was a delightful composite letter which the
happy trio concocted to send to Ellen Nussey, whose fate
it so often was to stay at home. This letter, which includes
the earliest of Mary Taylor's letters to survive, gives a vivid
picture of Madame Goussaert's schoolroom.

LETTER 2

*Mary and Martha Taylor and Charlotte Brontë to Ellen
Nussey, March-April 1842, WS no. 130; text from MS. in
Pierpont Morgan Library, New York.*

(This composite letter from Mary and Martha Taylor and
Charlotte Brontë to Ellen Nussey is on one large sheet of
paper, folded in the middle so as to produce two pages.
Mary began the letter, filling recto and verso of the first page,
but putting neither signature nor date. Charlotte then continued 'on this side' of Mary's letter, i.e. on the recto of the
second page, on 26 March; Martha finished up the page with
her note on 4 April. On the verso of this page, Mary then
added a note dated 5 April, followed by Martha's further
message, not dated.)

My Dear Ellen
    Do not think that I have forgotten you because I have so
many things to do that I can no more write to you now and
then, than I used to be able to run down to Brookroyd every

other day. As for Miss Brontë, I have not seen her since I
came here so you may judge that I do not spend my time
just as /I/ like. Before breakfast I draw, after breakfast I
practise, say German lessons and *draw*, after dinner walk
out, learn German and *draw*. [I] go to bed sometimes at nine
o'clock heartily tired and without a word to throw at any
one. If it were not Sunday I could not write to you fortunately the weather is too wet for us to go to church so I have
time for everything. In the enumeration of my employments
I have forgotten the writing of French compositions. This is
the plague of Koekleberg[1] schoolroom. "Avez vous fait
votre composition"? "Oui, mais je ne puis pas—*put a beginning to it.*" "Pouvez-vous m'aider"? Silence! What's the
french for *invite*? "It is eight *hours*! *When* shall we have the
tea? How many years have you?" this is a french girl talking
English—the Germans make an equal mess of both languages the german teacher worst of all. I must now tell you of
our teachers. Miss Evans is a well educated Englishwoman
who has been eight years in France whom I should like very
well if she were not so outrageously civil that I every now
and then suspect her of hypocrisy. The french teacher we
have not yet got so I can tell you nothing of her except that
she is coming in a few days (which she has been doing ever
since Christmas). Madame Ferdinand the music-mistress is
[a] little thin, black, talkative French woman. Monsieur her
husband a tall broad shouldered man with a tremendous
mouth who /is/ constantly telling his pupils that the voice
has but a very little hole to get out at and that there are
both tongue and teeth to interrupt it in its road and that the
orifice ought by all means to be opened as wide as possible
—Then comes Ms Gauné, a little black old Frenchman with
his history written on his face and a queer one it is—I speak
either of the face or the history—which you please. He has a
good appreciation of the literature of his country and speaks
some curious English. I think him a good master—Mons.
Huard—the drawing-master is a man of some talent, a good
judgment, and an intelligible manner of teaching he would

[1] Thus in MS. The Taylor girls' French, capitalization, etc, have
been left untouched throughout this letter.

be my favourite if he did not smell so of bad tobacco. Last and least is Mons. Scieré not that he appears to me to want sense and being a dancing master he ought not to want manner—but he has the faults of a french puppy, and they make it advisable never to exchange more words with him than the everlasting "Oui Monsieur—Non, Monsieur"—Martha is considerably improved. I can't put out my feet—"Allongez!—plus long! more!" All our awkwardnesses however are thrown into the shade by those of a belgian girl who does not know right foot from left and obstinately dances with her mouth open. There is also a Mons. Hisard, who makes strange noises in the back school room teaching gymnastics to some of the girls and I had nearly forgotten a grinning, dirty, gesticulating, belgian who teaches cosmography and says so often "Ainsi donc! c'est bien compris! n'est-ce pas?" that he has earned himself the names of Ainsi donc and Mr Globes. Amongst all this noise and bustle we have every possible opportunity of learning—if we choose. I must except French in which we make very little progress owing to the want of a governess. There are more English and Germans than French girls in the school consequently very little french is spoken and that little is bad. I will write no more till I have seen the Brontës.

                                        March—26th 1842
Dear Ellen—Mary Taylor says I am to write to you on this side of her letter—You will have heard that we have settled at Brussels instead of Lille—I think we have done well—we have got into a very good school—and are considerably comfortable—just now we are at Kokleberg[2] spending the day with Mary and Martha Taylor—to us such a happy day—for one's blood requires a little warming—it gets cold with living amongst strangers—You are not forgotten as you feared you would be. I will write another letter sometime and tell you how we are placed and amongst what sort of people —I[3] ⟨···⟩ Mary and Martha are not changed. I have a Catholic faith in them that they cannot change—Good-bye

[2] Thus in MS.
[3] Two words are thoroughly deleted here.

—remember me to your Mother and Mercy and write to me Ellen as soon as you can

C. Brontë.

April 4th 1842

Dear Ellen

I am to add my bit to this to this newspaper which you are to have sometime but no one knows when. We have had holiday for the last ten days and I don't feel at all inclined to begin lessons again. I am tired of this everlasting German and long for the day after to-morrow when our new French Mistress will come and we shall continue our French—I have the cousin of the Mr Jenkins[4] who took tea with my brother Joe at Brookroyd—sat by me, chattering like a magpie, and hoping it may be true that her cousin will come to Brussels before July. Mary is on the other side of me staring into a german dictionary, and looking as fierce as a tiger. There is a very sweet, ladylike, elegant girl here, who has undertaken to civilise our *dragon,* and she is actually improving a little under her hands! Would you like to be here cracking your head with French and german? by the way, you must excuse me if I send you some unintelligible english for in attempting to acquire other languages I have almost forgotten the little I knew of my own.

But I believe we are going to have prayers so I must put this away, but I will write some more some day. Good night.

Martha Taylor

Lest you should think yourself forgotten I take the first opportunity of sending you a letter—keep up your spirits and look forward to crossing the channel—sometime—Send me particular news of your Mother by my brothers and any thing else you may have to say.

April 5/42   Mary Taylor

and send me news about every one that I know. It is all the fashion for gentlemen to paint themselves, shall I send

[4] Rev. Jenkins, curate of Batley, or Rev. David Jenkins, of Pudsey.

you some paint for George.[5] When you see my brother Joe
have the kindness to pull him his hair right well for me and
give John a good pinch.

Remember me to your Mother and sisters, and believe me
to be still

Martha Taylor

A further glimpse of the Taylor girls at this time is provided by young Tom Dixon, who says in a letter (Leeds City
Museum) to his sister Mary, written in late April or early
May: 'There is nothing new here; the Koekelbergitesses did
not come to Church last Sunday so I can say nothing about
them except that on Wednesday last they were all quite well.
One of the young ladies will go over on the 8th of May so
you may expect a posse of letters fm them, with one or two
fm me, about 10th 11th or 12th. Remember me very kindly
to Joe and John.'

It was Martha who went across to Yorkshire, with her
brother John as escort. In June she wrote to Ellen two notes
which give an indication of their movements, and also of
some misunderstandings. A third letter, probably of this
time, is not dated.

LETTER 3

*Martha Taylor to Ellen Nussey, 22 June 1842; text from WS
no. 135.*

Leeds, June 22nd, 1842.
My dear Ellen,—When Joe came to us at Ilkley last Sunday
he told me of the invitation you had given him for me to pass
a few days at Brookroyd and he also said he had explained
to you how it was out of my power to avail myself of your
kindness.

Now I am going to take a liberty, I propose to myself the
pleasure of spending a long day with you whilst I am at
Gomersal. I think of going to my Mother's house on Friday

---

[5] George Nussey, Ellen's brother.

if the day be fine, and if not on Monday. If I go on Friday I shall be at church on Sunday, and then I hope I shall see you and if I don't go until Monday, I will let you know.

I will tell you all about Miss Brontës and my sister when I see you. Remember me kindly to your Mother and sister and believe me, my dear Ellen, Yours very affectionately,

Martha Taylor.

LETTER 4

Martha Taylor to Ellen Nussey, 24 June [?1842], not previously published; text from MS. in Berg Collection, New York Public Library.

My dear Ellen

I can't imagine what crochet you have got in your head, what can make you think I am angry with you.

I have been expecting you to call upon me to fix the day for me to spend with you. Perhaps you are in the right not to come to the house—I shall possibly come to see you to-morrow—when "you come", do you mean for a whole day or a call.

I can come any day but next Monday or Sunday excepting tomorrow. If it will suit you for me to come and spend the day with you on Thursday I will do so.

Now is it understood if I hear nothing more from you I will come in good time on Thursday morning and spend a very *long* day with you. I remain

in everything

M

June 24th.

[i.e. Martha, as noted by EN on the envelope]

LETTER 5

Martha Taylor to Ellen Nussey, not dated, but from contents 1841-42; not previously published; text from MS. in Berg Collection, New York Public Library.

My dear Ellen

I have come here this afternoon and I want you to come and spend the day with me tomorrow—now don't refuse me, it is almost the only day I have for I am only going to spend three or four days at Hunsworth.

I can suggest no means of bringing you here, but if you will walk there is plenty of room for you to remain all night and then you will be able to walk back on Wednesday morning.

Remember me kindly to your Mother and sister and believe me my dear Ellen

Yours affectionately
Martha Taylor —

Hunsworth Monday.

By August, Joseph and John Taylor were properly settled in at Hunsworth Mills cottage, and a family 'housewarming' was planned while Martha was staying with the Dixons in Leeds. Uncle Abraham was over for a summer visit to his home at 35 Springfield Place, where his sister-in-law 'Aunt Sarah' Taylor was in charge. Martha wrote on the 19th to invite Ellen Nussey to the festivity. It is clear that George Dixon (of Birmingham) was to squire her back across the Channel the following week, so Ellen was again warned to bring with her any letters that she had for transmission to Mary and Charlotte.

LETTER 6

Martha Taylor to Ellen Nussey, 19 August 1842, WS no. 141; text from MS. in Berg Collection, New York Public Library.

My dear Ellen—

We have just returned from Leeds where we have fixed that we will have the house warmed next Wednesday and my cousins, my Uncle and my Aunt Sarah are coming over—My brothers and I shall be exceedingly gratified if you, your sister Mercy, and your brothers, will come to tea on that day to meet them. Now will you come? or will you be stupid as you were about going to Brier Hall,[1] and if you refuse you will make me seriously angry with you—and you had better not, or I will tell all kinds of things of you to Miss Brontë.

We leave here for Birmingham on Thursday next so you must bring your letters with you.

> I remain conditionally
> Yours Truly
> Martha Taylor.

Hunsworth Mills. Friday Augst. 19—42

By September, Mary and Martha were settled in again at Koekelberg. Two of Mary's letters survive from this autumn term, before Martha's death in October.

LETTER 7

Mary Taylor to Ellen Nussey; not dated, but written in Brussels prior to October 1842, WS no. 138; text from MS. in Miriam Lutcher Stark Library, University of Texas.

Dear Ellen   It is very fortunate that you did not quarrel with the first half of your letter to such a point as to put it absolutely out of the world as I should thereby have lost very considerably, as I think it the best half of the two.

The lady who resides at some place illegible, had a daughter here named Isabella Simpson a very superior girl, but she has left and I shall probably never see her any more. As to what you say about reading, I think you are quite in the right to read all that falls into your hands; improving yourself does not consist in cramming your head with good sayings out of good books; you can never live exclusively with good people or read exclusively good works. You ought

[1] The Swaine family lived at Brier Hall (Cadman, pp. 75-7).

therefore to get into the habit of exercising your judgement
on every thing, book, word, or action that falls in your way
—beginning with a certain letter that you happen to be reading. There are two mistakes in the opinion you express as to
the superiority of one sex over the other. 1st superiority does
not consist in book learning and for proof I would take your
opinion on almost any subject in preference to your brother
Joshua's[1] though he no doubt has read as much as you and
I put together, and a little bit of Charlotte included.

You will see by Charlotte's letter[2] that you are not likely
to have your heart rejoiced by her presence. I am sorry for
your sake but not for any other reason. I intend to follow
her example myself as speedily as possible; and sincerely
hope I have bid adieu to your confounded 'patrie' (my own
though it be) for ever and a day. The stones will turn
another side towards me when I *do* come back again and
if anything looks at me with its old face I'll knock its teeth
down its throat.—Always excepting Ellen Nussey who may
look at me with any face she likes. I except also the Carrs[3]
who have been very kind to Martha and who knew my
Father. I except also Mrs Nussey, Mrs Cockhill[4] and Hannah
and of all the rest of Birstall parish I can buy the affection
—when I am rich enough.

Where in the name of the grand dieu de la foudre (a
Koekleberg expression) (it means Jupiter) did you find or
steal the description of New Zealand? I never *knew* anything about the country—which however does not prevent
my having described it in some overflow of poetic frensy—
if this be the case pray refer me to the volume of my works
in which it is to be found—or at least mention the date of
the night on which I dreamed it—

What do you think of Germany instead of New Zealand?
I have heard they are nice and savage there too—The few
specimens we have here are tamed the[y] still however in-

---

[1] Joshua Nussey, 1798-1871, Vicar of Oundle.

[2] Obviously enclosed with Mary's ; if it is WS no. 137, then Mary's
    letter can be dated as July.

[3] The solicitor Carrs, see Table E.

[4] The correct spelling is Cockill ; see Table D.

dulge in certain barbarous habits, such as eating enormously, with their mouths open putting both elbows on the table to guard their plate wearing seventeen petticoats (more or less) speaking the truth in the silliest manner possible even to their own disadvantage. Very different are the dapper frenchmen and assuming french women whom we English have the discrimination to imitate. They practise civility ie. tell lies till it is only the very wise ones among them that know[5] what the truth is and they take good care not to tell it.—dieu de la foudre, what's my paper done for?

Adieu My dear Ellen your are as near to me or nearer than when I could see you every day

Mary Taylor.

LETTER 8

Mary Taylor to Ellen Nussey; not dated, but annotated, probably by EN, '24 Sep 1842', WS no. 142; text from MS. in Miriam Lutcher Stark Library, University of Texas.

Dear Ellen

I did not write to you by Joe because I had two other letters to write during the busy time he staid with us. I think it very likely however that you will get this letter before Joe arrives as there is no knowing where he will run about to, before he set[s] off home.

I thank you for your chain—I will wear it the moment I want one, and will always hold it ready, for that occasion. I have even some idea of cutting a sly hole in the one I now wear in order to get at this one so much the sooner.

I thank you next for writing to me; to find the same hearty old English expressions of kindness that I know as old friends. There are plenty of goods here, but I have not tried them so often nor found them so sincere.

In the picture you draw to yourself of the pleasures and advantages of Koekleberg life put in a few colours that I will

---

[5] 'turn over' is inserted at this point, the end of the page. The remainder of the letter is squeezed in above the beginning on the first page, which may account for the mistake "your are'.

give you.—A falsehood you can never get to the bottom of.[1]
(There are exceptions.) An artificial kind of life that pre-
vents you from ever enjoying any simple or natural pleasures. The continually finding yourself suspected of the same
falsehood that all around you are guilty of—but what's the
use of grumbling when I'm going away? Going! Going! in to
the heart of Germany, /near/ to a place called Iserlohn.[2]
There is not another English person within a days journey,
nor I think a French one. There are plenty of mountains
trees and water and (I hope) of children to whom I can
teach English. How this turns out I will tell you when I have
been there a little time. I am invited to pass the winter with
Mde Schmidt a German lady[3] who has a daughter at Koekleberg; so that I shall not be frozen to death in the cold weather and when it grows warm I must "fend for myself."
Charlotte and Emily are well; not only in health but in mind
and hope. They are content with their present position and
even gay and I think they do quite right not to return to
England though one of them at least[4] could earn more at the
beautiful town of Bradford than she is now doing.

Excuse me writing any very sensible reasons for this decision first because I am listening to[5] a lecture in french while
I am writing to you in English—and 2ly because if you can't
see or rather feel why they are right I could not make you
understand them. It is a matter of taste and feeling, and I
think you feel pent up enough where you are to see why they
are right in staying outside the cage—though it is somewhat
cold.

Cold or warm farewell. I am going to shut my eyes for a
cold plunge—when I come up again I [will] tell you all what
its like.

                                    Mary Taylor.

[1] Mary's comments on this in both letters may be compared with
   Charlotte's account of Belgian schoolgirls in *The Professor*, chapter 12, and *Villette*, chapters 8 and 9.
[2] Mary finally went to Hagen.
[3] cf Abraham Dixon's letter, on p. 52.
[4] Mary wrote 'at Leeds', then *del*. 'Leeds'.
[5] Mary wrote 'to to', evidence of her difficulty in concentrating.

Alas, before Mary could plunge off to Germany, Martha was taken ill with what was probably cholera, and died on 12 October. She was buried in the Protestant Cemetery on the Chaussée de Louvain, outside the city. Mary went away into Brussels to stay with the Dixons, and wrote to Ellen three weeks later.

LETTER 9

Mary Taylor to Ellen Nussey, 1 November 1842, WS no. 145; text from MS. in Berg Collection, New York Public Library.

My dear Ellen

You will have heard by this time the end of poor Martha; and with my head full of this event and still having no thing to say upon it, or rather not feeling inclined to say it, I scarcely know why I write to you. But I don't wish you to think that this misfortune will make me forget you more than the rest did; having the opportunity of sending you a letter postage free I just write to tell you I think of you. You will wish to hear the history of Martha's illness—I will give you it in a few months if you have not heard it then; till then you must excuse me. A thousand times I have reviewed the minutest circumstances of it but I cannot without great difficulty give a regular account of them.—There is nothing to regret, nothing to recall—not even Martha.—She is better where she is—But when I recall the sufferings that have purified her my heart aches—I can't help it and every trivial accident sad or pleasant reminds me of her and of what she went through.

I am going to walk with Charlotte and Emily to the protestant cemetery this afternoon (Sunday 20 Oct)[1] It is long since I have seen them and we shall have much to say to each other. I am now staying with the Dixons in Brussels. I find them very different to what I expected. They are the

[1] The date should be 30 October. Charlotte referred to this visit to the cemetery in WS no. 147, *Shirley* chapter 23, and *The Professor* chapter 19.

most united affectionate family I ever met with. They have taken me as one of themselves and made me such a comfortable happy home that I should like to live here all my life.

This I could do if I had not a counter liking (so consistent we are!) to go into Germany and another to live at Hunsworth. I have finally chosen to go to Germany—activity being in my opinion the most desirable state of existence— both for my spirits, health, and advantage. I shall finish my letter after I have seen Charlotte. Well I have seen her and Emily. We have walked about six miles to see the cemetery and the country round it. We then spent a pleasant evening with my cousins and in presence of my Uncle and Emily one not speaking at all; the other once or twice. I like to hear from you. and thank you very much for your letter. Remember me to your sister Mercy and your Mother, and to all who inquire about me, if you think they do it more from kindness than curiosity. To Miss Cockhill[2] Mary and all the Misses Wooler, particularly to Miss Wooler, Miss Bradbury and the Healds.[3]

Mary Taylor.
11 Rue de la Regence[4]
1 Novbr 1842

If this letter should not reach you for some time after the date, it will not be because it has been delayed on the road but because an opportunity did not occur of sending it sooner by a private hand.

Mary Dixon wishes me to begin again to express her kind remembrances to you and your sister.

Soon after this, the Brontë girls were called home by the death of Aunt Branwell. Charlotte wrote to Ellen on 10 November from Haworth (WS no. 147).

[2] Cockill, ie Hannah, daughter of Thomas Cockill. See Table D. Mary deleted 'Tho' before 'Cockhill'.
[3] Mary Carr, of the solicitor's family, who in 1844 married the Rev. W. M. Heald, Vicar of Birstall. 'The Healds' are the Vicar and his sisters Harriet and Mary. Miss Bradbury is often mentioned by CB. See Tables D and E.
[4] Thus in MS. Mary's spelling of proper names is unreliable.

Martha Taylor's illness was unknown to me till the day before she died. I hastened to Kockleberg the next morning—unconscious that she was in great danger—and was told that it was finished. She had died in the night. Mary was taken away to Bruxelles. I have seen Mary frequently since. She is in no ways crushed by the event; but while Martha was ill she was to her more than a mother—more than a sister: watching, nursing, cherishing her so tenderly, so unweariedly. She appears calm and serious now: no bursts of violent emotion, no exaggeration of distress. I have seen Martha's grave—the place where her ashes lie in a foreign country. Aunt, Martha Taylor, and Mr. Weightman are now all gone; how dreary and void everything seems. Mr. Weightman's illness was exactly what Martha's was—he was ill the same length of time and died in the same manner. Aunt's disease was internal obstruction; she also was ill a fortnight.

At the end of 1842, Mary went off to Germany as originally planned. Charlotte visited the home-bound Ellen at Brookroyd for a few weeks, and then returned to Brussels without Emily, at the end of January 1843. Mary Taylor alerted the Dixons, who made further friendly overtures, Mary Dixon in particular offering a welcome. Charlotte told Ellen on 30 January (WS no. 152): 'Miss Dixon called this afternoon. Mary Taylor had told her I should be in Brussels the last week in January. You can tell Joe Taylor she looks very elegant and ladylike'. On 6 March she reported that she had been twice to the Dixons, who were 'very kind'. Mary Dixon, indeed, had conceived the idea of doing Charlotte's portrait to send to Mary Taylor in Germany. Charlotte's view of Mary's probable reaction to the gift is of considerable interest. The letter, which is in the Berg Collection, is not dated, but must have been written between 30 January and June 1843 (when Mary Dixon left Brussels).

. . . . I surrender my unfortunate head to you with resignation—the features thereof may yield good prac-

tice as they never yet submitted to any line of regularity
—but have manifested such a spirit of independence,
edifying to behold—You are mistaken however in your
benevolent idea that my portrait will yield pleasure to
Mary Taylor—do not give it to her, or if you do—do
not expect thanks in return—she likes me well enough
—but my face she can dispense with—and would tell
you so in her own sincere and truthful language if you
asked her.

The full letter is printed in Gérin, p. 219, but with several
errors of transcription; there is a P.S., 'I send a letter for
Mary to be enclosed in your packet.'
From Germany, Mary Taylor wrote both to Ellen and
to Charlotte. Her letters to Charlotte have not survived, but
Charlotte passed on the news in them to Ellen. On 6 March,
she wrote 'I have had two letters from Mary. She does not
tell me she has been ill, and she does not complain; but her
letters are not the letters of a person in the enjoyment of
great happiness' (WS no. 154). And in April, there is the
comment that Mary's 'resolute and intrepid proceedings',
teaching English to German boys, are 'very rational' (WS
no. 155).
To Ellen, Mary sent some lively budgets. The first is dated
16 February, 1843.

LETTER 10

*Mary Taylor to Ellen Nussey, 16 February 1843, WS no.
153; text from MS. in Berg Collection, New York Public
Library.*

Dear Ellen
   Your descriptions and opinions of the Miss Woolers etc
etc are more interesting than you imagine. Why do you not
send me some more of them? It is something very *interesting,*
to me [to] hear the remarks exclamations etc that people
make when they see any one from 'foreign parts'. I know
well how you would spend the month you talk of when Miss

Brontë was with you and how you would discuss all imaginable topics and all imaginable people all day and half the night. Tell me something about Emily Brontë. I can't imagine how the newly acquired qualities can *fit in,* in the same head and heart that is occupied by the old ones. Imagine Emily turning over prints or "taking wine" with any stupid fop and preserving her temper and politeness! Do you know your specimens of "people with good taste *who admire* The *Sea*" shocks me by its vulgarity. The Sea is but a simple air! You should admire *elaborate fantasias* made on elaborate *subjects* that want three hands or 12 fingers to play them— when you are left to invent now and then a "brilliant appogiatura, Cadence, Harpenspiel or what not to modulate through the fifth in to the next key or from a minor seventh close to—the devil knows what!

—If you can't understand it all remember I've been learning German, and how is it possible to keep ones brains [in] this land of Swedenborg, philosophy, abstract ideas and—*cabbage.* This last word is a literal translation of a German one always applied to anything very confused—my letter for instance.—However I thrive with it all. I am decidedly better —better than I have been since I left England and Brussels, or perhaps my moral condition there did not agree with me. I felt overpowered with weakness now I am cheerful and active. Do not think if I don't write to you often that I forget you. I write a public letter which I hope you see, and when I have written all the news I have what can I put in your letter? I will wait a day or two and if I find a great secret I will put it at the bottom of this page.—

Mary T.

I find nothing to say, that I have not said in the public letter and I must close my packet today for fear an estafette comes to know why I don't write. I have heard from Charlotte since her arrival she seems *content* at least but fear her sister's absence [may] have a bad effect. When people have so little amusement they cannot afford to lose any. However we sh[all] see.

Present my remembrances to Miss Heald[1] if she sent any to

[1] Sister of Rev. W. M. Heald, Vicar of Birstall.

me and I have really forgotten, and your letters are so
abominably written that I cannot afford time to read it over
again. Cannot you take pains and write neatly as I do? I
fully understand your regrets at being forced to remain at
home but there is always your Mother for a reason and perhaps if you left her you might regret as much that you had
not remained by her. Remember me to her and your sister
Miss Woole[r and] the Cockhills.

Mary Taylor
Feby 16 1843

Ovinstradt[2]

At the end of May, Joseph Taylor crossed to Europe
again, and he and Mary went touring together (WS no. 157),
Lambach in Austria (a health resort near Salzburg) being
included in the itinerary.

LETTER 11

*Mary Taylor to Ellen Nussey, 25 June 1843, not previously
published; text from MS. in Miriam Lutcher Stark Library,
University of Texas. The postmark on receipt is 'Leeds Jy
22 1843'.*

Dear Ellen
        Your brioche[1] came to hand just after I had got my
sofa; I had been wishing for such a thing for a fortnight
before, and should have wished for it for some months
longer if I had been obliged to wait till I got it myself. I
don't intend to use it for a footstool because I don't usually
wear satin shoes nor yet to set it before my pupils because
they are already rather soft,—as soft as the cushion and I
think the diet would not agree with them. I am sorry you
will not get this letter by Joe;[2] I had intended you should but

[2] Not traced ; possibly a misspelling.
[1] Apparently Mary means a cushion.
[2] cf the next letter.

I find myself so tired after a day's travelling that I should make a very sleepy production if I began to write when settled in my own room at the end of the day. I have already scribbled half-a-dozen sheets and Joe leaves me tomorrow.— We have had a very pleasant expedition; you must go to Mrs Burnley[3] and ask her to give you an account of it. I will now tell you something about myself. I am better for my journey and I was well before—I wrote some such contradictory statement to my Mother and she answered me by telling [me] always to write *truth* when I write to her. I can give no explanation though there *is* at first sight an apparent contradiction in the two speeches. I am very busy. I have 42 lessons a week making 7 a day. I make more than I need to live on but then I can always spend it besides I wish to get so many pupils that I shan't care for quarrelling with a Jew. Not that I have any decided intention of doing so but I see that if I were to tell one or two of the lazy ones very coolly that I must inform their parents that the mo[ney] I received for teaching them was uselessly spent, since they learnt nothing such a speech would have great effect on the conduct of the remainder. I must however be able to follow it up by adding a few lessons latter [i.e., 'later']—"Mr Somebody I have already explained to you that you profit nothing by your present line of study as however you do not seem inclined to alter it I must decline the pleasure of your company at the next lesson." This speech would be a thunderstroke to the other two or three innocents in the class who would take especial care not to come under the same category. I am in hopes of being able to effect this "thunderstroke" shortly. Since my return I have heard of six lessons more a week making 8 a day—I shall soon have more than I want.—As to other faults of the pupils I have none to complain of. If they were not as slow as Germans (*and that is* slow *indeed*) they would be very "nice sharp lads". As it is however they are nice *dull* ones. When I am not engaged in teaching I am learning, Music and German, so that with

---

[3] The Burnleys had lived at Pollard Hall, next to the Red House, Gomersal, for three generations. In 1844 Thomas Burnley bought the estate and its fine old mansion, erected in 1659.

sewing (only what I can't help) walking out, seeing my
neighbours eating and sleeping I have not a moment to spare.
—Scarcely to write to you.—I am not surprised to hear that
Miss C. Wooler[4] has cut me dead. *Miss* Wooler should have
known better but she is timid and will probably come back
again if ever I should make my appearance in your parts.
I am very sorry to hear of Sarah Nussey's, to me, *sudden* illness.[5] They will certainly lose the "flower of the flock" in
losing her. All you say about the natives interests me very
much, particularly the Cockhills. What influence will this
unfortunate fever have on their school?[6] Is it not likely to
injure it? Martha's death though not from a contagious disorder has exceedingly affected Mde Gaussaert's school,
which I am very sorry for and would gladly repair if I
could.[7]

Either this or some other cause has so reduced the number of her pupils that she would be glad to take a few on
rather reduced terms—this of course it [i.e., 'is'] not to be
known, after the usual fashion of schools. A troublesome
sort of policy I dont at all approve of.—At Lambach We
saw Abram and Mary Dixon both so much better for the
cold water system that they recommended it to everyone.[8]

[4] Catherine Wooler. Miss Wooler did not approve of Mary's 'proceedings'.

[5] Sarah Nussey, daughter of John Nussey of White Lea, Batley, and
Ellen's second cousin, died on 21 July 1843, aged twenty-four. See
Table C.

[6] From this reference it is clear that Sarah Nussey, the cousin, was
a teacher at Mrs Thomas Cockill's school, which is shown in
Pigot's Directory for 1841 as at Oakwell Hall. In July 1844 (WS
no. 178) Charlotte refers to the school as 'Miss Cockill's'. The
Cockills and Nusseys were related. See Tables C and D.

[7] This sentence establishes Madame Goussaert (Mary's spelling of
names is unreliable) as the Directrice of the 'Château de Koekelberg'; in addition, the name of her husband, Norbert Goussaert,
is recorded as the informant on the death certificate of Martha
Taylor. See Appendix D.

[8] As a result of the work of Priessnitz (1799-1851), hydrotherapy
had become a very popular treatment at health resorts. Among
other ordeals it involved cold water packs to the body and bare-
foot promenades through dewy meadows. Lambach is in Austria,
between Linz and Salzburg.

I have heard that your brother George[9] was going to try it at Ilkley—if he does persuade him to take John[10] with him; from what I have heard it would do them both a great deal of goo[d]. The best news in your letter is that your sister does not object to your improving yourself by reading etc. I am glad she has picked up a little sense down in Sussex[11] and hope in a little time she will have learned not to exclude all the best, wittiest, and most sensible books because they are not *"serious"*.—Read away Ellen books of all sort and all characters. As you cannot leave home and see something of real life the next best thing is to *read* read read. Not with the stupid idea that you are to imitate all you read. When you read a bad book it it [i.e., 'is'] like making acquaintance with a bad man—you do not do it to imitate him but *to know him*. After a little examination you will find that there is something bad in all and the idea of picking out a few as the exclusively good ones, and that because they treat of religious subjects is stupid enough to be worthy of the narrowness of Birstal "little flock."[12] You say nothing of the Brookes of Dewsbury;[13] I conclude therefore you had nothing to say. Give my love to those who inquire after me. particularly to your Mother and sisters and the Bradburys.

/I have just received from John the news of your sister's death[14] Be comforted in this gloomy hour by the reflection of the care and kindness she received from you.[15]/

9 George Nussey, Ellen's brother, had suffered a breakdown, which ultimately proved to be mental trouble.

10 John Taylor, Mary's brother.

11 Mercy Nussey had been staying with her brother Henry in his Rectory near Chichester.

12 There were several little sects of Dissenters in the Gomersal and Birstall area.

13 Leah and Maria Brooke, daughters of John Brooke of Dewsbury, had been at Roe Head with Mary and Charlotte. Brooke was an old friend of the Rev. Patrick Brontë, and was partner in the banking firm of Halliley, Son and Brooke (WS no. 33).

14 Ellen's sister, Sarah Walker Nussey, who had been in ill-health for many years, died on 16 June 1843, aged 33.

15 The passage from 'I have just' to 'from you' has been inserted in narrow space at the first fold. The letter continues normally below the second fold.

I have nothing to say of this little place which will interest you. I am slowly making acquaintance. Some are stupid some silly some sensible—not many though—Many of them blessed with the same narrow notions that exist in all small communities when the members of them get no ideas from without—None of them are equal to some old friends I left behind to whom believe me true as ever.

Mary Taylor.

25th June

Next there is a lively account of Mary's lessons in Hagen with Friedrich Hallé, father of Sir Charles Hallé. The old man was noted for his admiration of Beethoven. The letter is not dated, but seems to have been written in winter, or at the earliest late autumn.

LETTER 12

Mary Taylor to Ellen Nussey, not dated, but written at Hagen in the winter of 1843; not previously published; text from MS. in Berg Collection, New York Public Library.

Dear Ellen

I have just been reading 6 or 7 letters to which I *should* have written answers when Joe was here, and have taken yours to occupy this spare hour because I see I am two in your debt. I expect you are by this time safe back in the old nest in the hillside and without bright youths to attend to who smoke cigars in bed and strengthen the sugar with cayenne. In your next you must tell me some Birstall news— some real scandal—from Mrs Williams[1] or such like. I can however give no return in kind that would interest you because I know very little of the people and *you* nothing at all. Then all Hagen is related and the relations only quarrel amongst themselves without betraying each other to stran-

---

[1] Not traced.

Plate 1

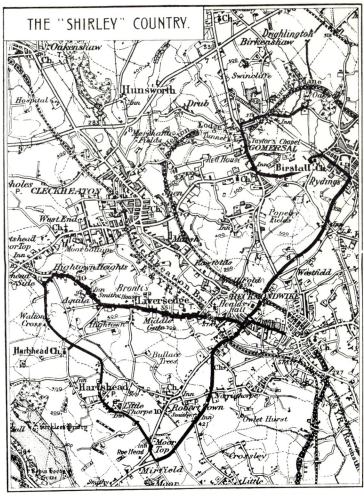

The HEAVY LINE shows the Route taken by the Brontë Society on their Excursion through the "Shirley" Country.

SCALE—2 inches to a mile.

The *Shirley* Country

gers. I have read a French novel called Consuelo[2] which I admire exceedingly was that the one you spoke of? if so you would not have given yourself too much trouble if you had learned French for the express purpose of reading it. You are too critical.—I have spoken first of this because it is the thing that has interested me most in the last month. The next things are my flowers, that is some green stuff in pots which *is* to bloom sometime. You cannot imagine nor can I explain the pleasure they give me. I am filled with wonder when I see my tulip bud getting red and my kali (which has been in the family way 2 months) shewing some white. These are nothing however to what I shall see when I *go loose* (German for have my way) in a garden, as I intend to have next summer. After the flowers some music. This is interesting in itself and the enthusiastic temperament of my master make[s] it more so. It is pleasant after commonplace compliments and cut and dried wit, to begin such a conversation as this.

Na! Good morning you aren't frozen dead then?—Good morning Mr Halle—Na! We'll try the new Sonata, now put some strength into your hands (when I've played three lines) Na! do you see anything in it? Yes—Yes! (looking as if he'd like to shake me) Yes!—Perhaps you know a better! perhaps the man doesn't please you! Do you think there ever was a better composer in the world?—How should I know?—Why then I tell you! you may ask all over the world and you can't find one, but what's the use of seeking? Lord to whom shall we go? thou hast the words of eternal life! and when this Sonata does not go to Heaven I'll stay outside with St. Peter! Na! Play it again! That cursed F. the piano is worth nothing. Will you lift your hands? Why fall asleep then quietly! Herr Halle why could'n't the[3] man write b instead of c flat?—Because he didn't want to write nonsense!—Nonsense! It's just the same note!—Can you count five?—Yes in English.—No you can't!—Well if I can't what

---

[2] Novel by George Sand, published February 1842 - March 1843 in *La Revue Independente,* and then in 8 vols.

[3] Mary wrote 'the the', and spelt 'Halle' thus, as well as 'you'r' following.

has that to do with this b instead of c. Would you write b instead of c there? Yes why not? Many thanks for your kindness, I won't come to you'r concert. But tell me then! Find it out! Then follows a very sensible explanation; Then some more enthusiastic praise of Beethoven. A remark that people like Herr Moll[4] who don't like music are oxen—an eternally repeated anecdote of Beethoven and *a little* attention to what I profess to be learning. I assure you there is a peculiar pleasure in hearing one's self called an ox. It is something utterly original. The man has considerable musical knowledge and when I don't vex him by not admiring Beethoven, can give valuable instruction. After music comes algebra. I can say nothing of this except that I like it partly I believe because it is odd in a woman to learn it, and I like to establish my right to be doing odd things.—Give my love to your Mother and sisters.

[no signature]

By October of this year, 1843, there had been among Mary's friends a great deal of discussion of her 'resolute proceedings'. Charlotte had this to say, on 13 October (WS no. 165; text from MS. in Huntington Library):

Mary Taylor is getting on well—as she deserves [to]—I often hear from her—her letters and yours are one of my few pleasures—she urges me very much to leave Brussels and go to her—but at present however tempted to take such a step I should not feel justified in doing so—To leave a certainty for a complete uncertainty would be to the last degree imprudent. Notwithstanding Brussels is indeed desolate to me now—since Mary Dixon left I have had no friend . . . . Mr George Dixon will take this letter to England.

Another letter a few days later touches on the matter of Joseph Taylor's inclination to Ellen (cf WS nos. 150, 151),

---

[4] Not traced.

and comments admirably on Mary Taylor's energy and independence.

(MS., Pierpont Morgan Library (Bonnell Collection), New York. Dated by Ellen Nussey 'Brussels 1843', and written shortly after 13 October (Dr Mildred Christian's dating), not 15 November as given in WS no. 166).

[Extract 1] I think Joe Taylor is looking very well—but that family always have colour—you are foolish to be so reluctant to go to Hunsworth—go—and don't be ashamed to say that you like Joe Taylor—he is worthy of being liked and admired also—which few men are— as for being desperately in love that is another thing— [Extract 2] I do not give to the (I am forced to take a pencil my pen is unmanageable) I say I do not give to the step Mary Taylor has taken the unqualified approbation you do—It is a step proving an energetic and active mind, proving the possession of courage, independence—talent, but it is not a *prudent* step—Often genius like Mary's triumphs over every obstacle without the aid of prudence—and she may be successful— hitherto she is so—but opinion and custom run so strongly against what she does—that I see there is danger of her having much uneasiness to suffer—if her pupils had been girls, it would be all well—the fact of their being BOYS /or rather young men/ is the stumbling-block—This opinion is for YOU only mind—[1]

Throughout the year 1843, Charlotte's unhappiness at the Pensionnat Heger had been increasing and she returned home at the end of December. At this point, a letter written by Mary Taylor's uncle Abraham Dixon has some valuable

[1] Later in this letter WS misread a name, printing 'Taylor' instead of 'Allbutt' in this sentence: 'She [Madame Heger] is a reasonable and calm woman but Nelly as to warmheartedness she has as much of that article as Mrs Allbutt' [i.e., Marianne, sister of Miss Wooler, who married Rev. T. Allbutt in 1835.] This mistaken reading has been used by biographers to support unfavourable comments on Mary Taylor's mother.

information to offer. He is writing to his daughter Mary
(Leeds City Museum).

                                        Brussels 30 Dec 1843
My Dear Mary,
    I received your very short letter dated Ilkley 28 Sep.
this I send by Miss Brontë who leaves on Sunday for
her home and does not mean to return.
    Sometime since I requested Henry to ask Aunt's[1]
Chapman and Sarah if they would like to live in
Ostend, but he has never informed me.[2] . . . .
    Madame Goussaert has gone at this unseasonable
season to take a tour in Germany and visit Madame
Schmidt and of course Mary Taylor. I hear nothing yet
of Joe's arrival here. Miss Evans[3] told me that he had
written he would be here on the 20th Decr—perhaps he
may have been and gone off with Madame G—! . . . .
Louisa[4] the youngest dined at Mr Jenkins's on Xmas
Day along with Miss Brontë and others with myself
. . . . I may mention that the house at Ostend is quite
large enough for you, Aunts C and S, Ellen Taylor and
myself—

Early in April 1844, Mary Taylor herself returned, in
what Charlotte described as a 'sudden change of plan' (WS
no. 173), and Ellen Nussey promptly sent her a welcome,
which Mary acknowledged as follows. (She had been with
George Dixon at Chad Road, in the Edgbaston district of
Birmingham.)

---

[1] Thus in MS. Mary Chapman and Sarah Taylor, sisters of Laetitia
    Dixon, and aunts, therefore, of Mary Dixon. See Table A.
[2] Henry Taylor had by this time left Brussels.
[3] Senior teacher at Koekelberg, cf Letter 2.
[4] Louisa Bright, possibly the cousin of Mr Jenkins mentioned in
    Letter 2.

LETTER 13

Mary Taylor to Ellen Nussey, postmark Leeds 13 April
[1844], SLL no. 136; text from MS. in Berg Collection, New
York Public Library.

Dear Ellen
  Many thanks for your welcome to England—How did
you smell out so speedily that I was come? I shall see you
and ask you this and a thousand other questions in about a
fortnight and then I hope to see C.B. too. I am going to
stretch the house at Hunsworth and make it hold three or
four people to sleep whereas I understand that now it only
holds two (strangers). Wish M. Carr much happiness for
me, she will be married before I see her again.[1] I have nothing to write and live in hopes of seeing you so I will not
crack my brain to find anything.
  Remember me to your Mama and Sisters.
                                          Yours   M. Taylor.
          Chad Road   April . . . 44

  Soon, the three friends had a delightful reunion, which
Ellen retailed to her friend Mary Gorham on 21 May.

  . . . . Mary Taylor has been staying with her brothers
4 miles from here—I said my adieu to her last night—
She crosses the German Ocean again tomorrow. Miss
Brontë has been a few days with Mary—I have been a
good deal there too, and had the satisfaction of meeting
Mary in nearly every visit she made . . . . When I had
certain information of Mary's arrival I set off with my
youngest brother at 9 o'clock at night to see her, and
there I found Charlotte Brontë also, both, were talking
and talking with all their might in the garden, it was so
dark when I joined them that we could distinguish noth-

---

[1] Mary Carr (see Table E) married the Rev. W. M. Heald on 23
April 1844. He is portrayed as the curate, 'Rev. Cyril Hall', in
Shirley (WS no. 513).

ing but figures approaching and so afraid were we each
of saluting a wrong relationship that we cautiously
peered into each other's faces—then, all at once a 'bless
you' burst forth in all the power of friendship and affection.

One of Mary's brothers accompanies her to Germany
and they attend the great musical festival at Cologne
next week. [From the transcription by C. W. Hatfield,
Brontë Parsonage Museum.]

Mary returned to Germany that autumn, to which period
the following letter, though undated, must belong. The page
has been torn away, leaving many lines truncated.

LETTER 14

*Mary Taylor to Ellen Nussey, not dated, but written in
1844, SLL no. 135; text from MS. in Berg Collection, New
York Public Library.*

Dear Ellen

I am just now in a terribly talking humour, and if you
were here I should entertain you for hours with interesting
trifles;—interesting *to me* and if they were not so to you,
why you would have to bear it! But as I can't enter into a
long circumstantial explanation of the state of things here
and there is nothing important going forward I have just
nothing to say. I am alone and melancholy. We sometimes
take it into our heads—at least I do, to wonder what we live
for, to look all round and see nothing in this world worth
getting up for in the morning. I am particularly apt to be of
this opinion when something has occured[1] to show me that
those things which I value, those virtues I strive after, that
moral beauty which makes the charm [of ev]ery day life—
all that is worth living for in fact is despised ⟨···⟩ ted by
other people. This sometimes gives me the idea that ⟨···⟩
taken and always makes me feel alone in the world. ⟨···⟩

[1] Thus in MS.

very have I lately made. Persons whom I considered ⟨···⟩
their conduct that they had no more ⟨···⟩ sider Virtue and
morality than if they had me— ⟨···⟩ particulars cannot be
written or are not ⟨···⟩ you them when I see you, and if I
never tell ⟨···⟩ self the repetition of a vexatious history.
⟨···⟩ you when my *outlandish* friends de- ⟨···⟩ what Charlotte is doing. I think of her too. ⟨···⟩—since I left England.
What is the ⟨···⟩ nervous? I have heard of your being⟨···⟩
you for a full account of her state of health and occupations.
I can easily imagine that she is grown low spirited with
solitude and want of interesting employment. Pray write—
write sooner than I have done to you and tell me how she
goes on. I half expect Joe this Autumn but if M. Dixon and
William come as they talk of doing, perhaps he will think
that is enough.[2] In any case write to me, particularly about
Miss Brontë. I have neglected writing to Miss Cockhill. Tell
her I will do it shortly. The reason is we have had neither
earthquake nor revolution here so I have nothing to say. My
own affairs go on as usual. I teach and practise music.—You
must have heard this till you are tired of it.

Yours truly,   M. Taylor.

The mood of dissatisfaction so obvious in this letter
culminated, by September, in a decision to resume the New
Zealand plan. On the 16th, Charlotte told Ellen the news
(WS no. 183): 'Mary Taylor is going to leave our hemi-
sphere. To me it is something as if a great planet fell out
of the sky. Yet, unless she marries in New Zealand, she
will not stay there long.' Mary, however, did not come back
from Germany at once. Charlotte was still speculating on her
date of return when she wrote to Ellen on 14 November
(WS no. 186): 'I wonder when Mary Taylor is expected in
England—it surprises me to hear of Joe being in Switzerland probably she is with him there also—in that case it may
yet be some weeks before they return—I trust you will be at
home—part of the time at least while she is at Hunsworth—

[2] Joseph Taylor, Mary Dixon, and her brother William Taylor
Dixon.

and that you she and I may meet again somewhere under the canopy of heaven—'. Mary had returned by early January 1845.

LETTER 15

Mary Taylor to Ellen Nussey, 4 January [1845], not previously published; text from MS. in Berg Collection, New York Public Library.

Dear Ellen

Here I am again and am very anxious to know how you are and how George is getting on. When shall I come and see you? Joe wishes to borrow George's gig and horse on Sunday night to go to Leeds on Monday morning. Could you not come in it or the day after? A. and T. Dixon[1] will be here on Sunday, to whom you will have nothing to say but the day following I shall be alone and very much want to see you I think a night from home would do you good if you could be spared so long.[2] Charlotte is very well she sends her love.

    Remember me to your Mother and Sisters
M. Taylor

       4 Jany.[3]

Mary had gone at once to Haworth 'looking very well' and 'in good spirits', as Charlotte reported (WS no. 187), but not bringing with her the hoped for letter from Monsieur Heger (WS no. 188). In early February, Charlotte paid a

---

[1] Abraham and Thomas Dixon.

[2] Ellen's brother George was ill.

[3] Mary at first put '5', then changed it to '4'. 4 January in 1845 was a Saturday. There are discrepancies of dating here, for Mary was clearly at Hunsworth when she wrote this letter, while she was clearly at Haworth when CB wrote letter no. 187 which WS conjecturally date Monday 6 January. Perhaps Mary had just *returned* from Haworth, and so can send CB's message in the penultimate sentence.

farewell visit to Hunsworth (WS no. 190). It was a desperately unhappy week, for Charlotte was assailed by her old enemy, nervous headache and sickness, and knew well enough, as Mary told Mrs Gaskell years later, that she was facing a frustrated and lonely future. Mary could not persuade her to leave home, though she tried her best. 'I told her very warmly that she ought not to stay at home; that to spend the next five years at home, in solitude and weak health, would ruin her; that she would never recover it. Such a dark shadow came over her face when I said, "Think of what you'll be five years hence!" that I stopped, and said, "Don't cry, Charlotte!" She did not cry, but went on walking up and down the room, and said in a little while, "But I intend to stay, Polly." (Extract 9 of first letter, Appendix B.)

It was indeed the last time that these two friends met 'under the canopy of heaven.'

And so Mary set off alone to the Antipodes. She sailed on the barque *Louisa Campbell,* leaving London on 18 March and Plymouth on 21 March, and arriving in Wellington on 24 July (*New Zealand Spectator, 26 July 1845*).

The first of her letters to survive from this new adventure was written three years later, in July 1848, and was prompted by the arrival of *Jane Eyre.* Her experiences in the interim are, however, reflected to some extent in the news of her exchanged by her friends at home. Here is Charlotte, to Ellen, on 2 April 1845 (WS no. 194; text from MS. in Huntington Library):

Mary Taylor finds herself free—and on that path for adventure and exertion to which she has so long been seeking admission—Sickness—Hardship—Danger are her fellow-travellers—her inseparable companions. She may have been out of the reach of these S.W. and N.W. gales before they began to blow—or they may have spent their fury on land and not ruffled the sea much— if it has been otherwise she has been sorely tossed while we have been sleeping in our beds or lying awake thinking about her.

Yet these real—material dangers /when once past/
leave in the mind the satisfaction of having struggled
with a difficulty and overcome it—Strength—Courage
—experience are their inevitable results— . . . . I repeat
then, that Mary Taylor has done well to go out to New
Zealand—but I wish we could soon have another letter
from her—I hope she may write from Madeira.

Mary's previous letter, mentioned here, had elicited from
Charlotte on 27 March the remark 'Mary is in her element
now. She has done right to go out to New Zealand' (WS
no. 193).
By 1 June there was more news, which Charlotte summarized for Ellen (WS no. 199; text from MS. in Brontë
Parsonage Museum).

You probably know that another letter has been received from Mary Taylor . . . . It was written at about
4° N. of the Equator—the first part of the letter contained an account of their landing at Santiago—Her
health at that time was very good—and her spirits
seemed excellent—they had had contrary winds at first
setting out but their voyage was then prosperous—In
the latter portion of the letter she complains of the
excessive heat and says she lives chiefly on oranges but
still she was well—and freer from head-ache and other
ailments than any other person on board—the receipt
of this letter will have relieved all her friends from a
weight of anxiety.

On 18th September, Charlotte wrote again (WS no. 214):

I have just read Mary's letters; they are very interesting,
and show the vigorous and original cast of her mind.
There is but one thing I could wish otherwise in them,
that is a certain tendency to flightiness—it is not safe,
it is not wise, and will often cause her to be miscon-
trued. Perhaps *flightiness* is not the right word, but it is

a devil-may-care tone; which I do not like when it proceeds from under a hat, and still less from under a bonnet. I long to hear of Mary being arrived at her remote destination and occupied in serious business, then she will be in her element; then her powerful faculties will be put to their right use.

On 31 December, there was 'a note from Ellen Taylor informing me that letters have been received from Mary and that she was well and in good spirits' (WS no. 222). On 23 January 1846, Charlotte noted 'Mary Taylor's letter was deeply interesting and strongly characteristic—it is one of those matters I hope to talk over with you, when I see you' (WS no. 223). There was mail at Hunsworth in May, while Charlotte and Ellen had news in August (WS nos. 251, 265). In September Charlotte wrote to Ellen (WS no. 267): 'By this time you will have got Mary's letters—most interesting they are—and she is in her element—because she is where she has a toilsome task to perform, an important improvement to effect—a weak vessel (Waring) to strengthen—She will remain in New Zealand as long as she can there find serious work to do—but no longer—'

Later that month, with reference to some fuss about new furniture at Hunsworth, Charlotte remarked (WS no. 270): 'I wonder what their sister Mary would say to them if they told her that tale? She sits on a wooden stool without a back in a log-house without a carpet—and neither is degraded nor thinks herself degraded by such poor accommodation.' Obviously Mary had given her friend a vivid account of Waring's colonial cottage.

The next news is in May 1847, when Charlotte put a note on the flap of an envelope to Ellen on the 5th: 'at last there is another letter from Mary Taylor. I send it to you, you are to return it to Hunsworth' (quoted Mildred Christian, 'Census'). A month later, on 5 June, there is another reference (WS no. 292; text from MS. in Huntington Library):

I return you Mary Taylor's letter—it made me somewhat sad to read it—for I fear she is no longer quite

content with her existence in New Zealand—she finds
it too barren—I believe she is more homesick than she
will confess—Her gloomy ideas respecting you and me
prove a state of mind far from gay—I have also received a letter—its tone was similar to your own—and
its contents too—an allusion or two to points on which
she enjoins secrecy but which concern herself alone—
prevent my sending it—you lose nothing, however—for
the two letters with that slight exception are nearly
alike— . . . .

December 1847 saw the arrival of more mail (WS no.
330): 'I had a letter from Mary Taylor last week—short
and without one word of news in it, except that she was in
better health and spirits than she had usually enjoyed in
Europe.'
In March 1848 there is a further reference to Mary's
health (WS no. 355): 'Mary Taylor too has more than once
been in the state you describe ['constant low fever in the
system']—she has however got the better of it—.'
Early in June 1848, Charlotte was visited at Haworth by
Joseph Taylor, his cousin William Henry Taylor, and
Henry's cousin Jane Dawson Mossman (see Table B), who
all drove over from Hunsworth 'to make some enquiries
respecting Mde Heger's school on account of Ellen Taylor'
(WS no. 379). This was, of course, not a new idea, having
been mooted as long ago as 1843. Nothing came of it, however. Charlotte noted that Henry Taylor strongly resembled
his cousin John Taylor, and that the trio had not had recent
mail from Mary.
There is one good budget of news, however, in a letter
which Charlotte wrote to Miss Wooler on 28 August, in
which she summarized the contents of Mary's recent letters
(WS no. 388; text from MS. in Allbutt Collection, Fitzwilliam Museum, Cambridge):

I heard from Mary Taylor in June: she wrote in excellent spirits; her proceedings seem prosperous, and she
says she is leading an active, happy and joyous life. She

had lately bought a cow, and had some thoughts of purchasing a section of land. She expressed pity for my comparatively dull, uneventful, and unoccupied existence. Her brother Waring was then on the point of being married—and I hear since that he is married—to a Miss Mary Knox, the daughter of a Dr Knox, an emigrant from Edinburgh (I shrewdly suspect him, by the way, to be no other than the Dr Knox of Hare and Burke notoriety). The lady is a Methodist, and very religious: Mary said that she supplied Waring with tracts, and was trying to convert him; she had prevailed on him to accompany her to chapel, but could not induce him to become a teacher in the Sunday School. Mary was not very sanguine about their prospects of permanent mutual happiness—she regards Waring as constitutionally hypochondriacal; perhaps, however, the change may do him good.

Waring Taylor's marriage, Dr Knox, etc, are discussed in the Introduction to Part III.

The rereading of these letters from Mary, with their remarks about Charlotte's 'comparatively dull, uneventful and unoccupied existence,' must have spurred Charlotte on to sit down the very next week, on 4 September, to write a long and brilliant letter refuting this view of her life. In this, the only letter of hers which Mary kept, she described the visit which she and Anne had paid two months previously to her publisher, George Smith, in London. Since this letter is the subject of comment in Mary's own letters, it is given in full in Appendix E.

Unfortunately, the version published by WS (no. 390) is grossly defective. C. K. Shorter first printed this mangled text in 1900, in his Haworth edition of the *Life*, as a footnote to the modified extract from the letter which Mrs Gaskell had used. Subsequently reprinted by WS without recourse to the original (then as now in the Manchester University Library), this shortened and altered version has been accepted by only too many Brontë scholars as the text

which Charlotte wrote. Perhaps George Smith himself dic-
tated its changes, for he himself published an account of
this dramatic first meeting in the *Cornhill Magazine,* 1900.
Obviously, however, Charlotte's version, written two months
after the great experience, is more likely to have the detailed
truth than Smith's, written fifty-two years later.[1]

And now we come to the first of Mary's letters from New
Zealand to survive. It will need an introduction by way of
background.

[1] The matter is fully discussed in my article, 'Woozles in Brontëland', *Studies in Bibliography,* 1971.

PART THREE

New Zealand

Mary arrived in New Zealand on 24 July 1845; her first surviving letter is dated 1 July 1848. In these three years, what had she done, how had she prospered? We have seen something of her at second hand through her friends' correspondence in England, but more remains to be traced on the New Zealand scene itself.

William Waring Taylor had arrived in Wellington in April 1842, and by 1843 was conducting a general business and importing agency, living in and trading from his wooden cottage on Herbert Street, Te Aro, not far from the waterfront. Te Aro was regarded as the commercial area of the settlement. At first Mary stayed with him, though not as Charlotte thought in a 'log-house'. It was the normal New Zealand affair of sawn timber, finished on the outside with overlapping weatherboards, such as may be seen in the photograph in Plate 5. Nor was it a mere makeshift, for it survived the earthquake of 1848 with only the loss of its chimney, when many more elaborate buildings crumbled to the ground.

In 1845 Wellington was a small settlement only five years old. It numbered, with its outlying areas, some 4,000 persons, of whom 2677 lived in the 'Town'. It was the first of the New Zealand Company settlements to be established in this

country, Colonel Wakefield negotiating the purchase of the
land round Port Nicholson in September and October 1839.
The *Cuba* with its party of surveyors arrived on 2 January
1840, but before anything much was done the first emigrants
arrived also, the pioneer vessel being the *Aurora* on 22 January. Hard on her heels came the *Oriental* on 31 January
with its contingent from Yorkshire, the *Duke of Roxburgh*
on 8 February (with James Greenwood aboard), and the
Bengal Merchant with its Scotsmen from the Clyde on 20
February. The settlers camped at first, in mercifully fine
weather, on the shingle banks at the mouth of the Hutt
River, on the north-eastern shore of the harbour, where the
Cuba party had decided to place their town, then thought of
as 'Britannia'. The vulnerability of this area to flooding
having been dramatically demonstrated, however, it was decided to move to the higher if more hilly terrain on the
south-western shore 'at the head of the bay'. The name was
changed to 'Wellington', and here in July 1840, after further
harassing delays, the Company's Surveyor finally completed
his work.

He offered the settlers a 'Town' surveyed into 1,100 sec-
tions of one acre each, threaded with some thirty miles of
paper 'streets', and backed by nearly a thousand acres of
public reserve lying in a ring still known as the 'Town Belt'.
The lots were selected according to the order of choice
established by the London ballot of the previous year, many,
of course, going to the London speculators. The settlement
became at once, therefore, rather scattered, and the 'Town',
though 'laid out', as Mary afterwards phrased it, was hap-
hazard in its development.

It began as a series of buildings in raupo, wood and brick,
strung out along the waterfront in two long crescents. See
the map on p. 68. The northern division, behind which
lay the undulating ground of Thorndon Flat, was 'the court
end of the town, being the neighbourhood of Government
House, the Church, Law Courts, Police Court, New Zealand
Company's Survey Office, etc' (Brees, p. 14). Its shoreline
was Lambton Quay, always spoken of as 'the Beach', which
curved away southwards, backed narrowly by the steep

Plate 2

Te Aro Flat, from Windy Point, 1842

Plate 3

Dixon Street

Dixon Street

Cuba Street

Mary Taylor's two-storeyed
building, with gable

Te Aro, with Thorndon beyond, 1851

cliffs of the Terrace, until it ended at the big bluff known as 'Clay' or 'Windy' Point.

Beyond this barrier, difficult to negotiate in rough weather or exceptional tides, the shoreline curved away again in a second crescent, backed this time by Te Aro Flat. A view of this area is shown in Plate 2, where the observer is standing on high ground somewhere in the Boulcott Street area and looking southward (Ward, p. 223). From its junction with Lambton Quay at Windy Point—at water level just below the flagstaff in Plate 2—Willis Street ran south under the edge of the hill. Manners Street curved off it halfway along, to run round eastwards, parallel to the shore line and not far from it, as indicated in the map on p. 68. Here were the wharves and their associated buildings; beyond this, the settlement petered out in the central swampy ground by the Maori pa, Taranaki (present-day Taranaki Street).

In Plate 2, the three raupo houses with thatched roofs in the foreground stand in Willis Street, which runs straight up to the right of the view. The wharf at which a substantial vessel lies is backed by the Custom House and Post Office, at the corner of Old Customhouse Street (Bond Street today, see Irvine-Smith p. 182) and Farish Street. In the Plate, two or three figures are to be seen strolling there. Beyond these buildings is the Exchange, with a 'classical' front, and yet further to the left is the wharf built by Capt. W. B. Rhodes at the foot of Cuba Street, then a mere cart track wandering inland to the unoccupied flats.

By 1845, traders established in this area included, besides Rhodes, the stock and station agents Bethune and Hunter, whose cattle yards were opposite Rhodes's store at the corner of Cuba and Manners Streets, while their store was nearby in Old Customhouse Street. In Farish Street were Dr Fitzherbert's stores and the Ordnance Stores. The Wesleyan Chapel stood in Manners Street, and the Military Hospital was in Sturdee Street, just the other side of Dixon Street.

It was here that Waring Taylor was established when Mary landed in 1845. His house was on the eastern side of Herbert Street, a one-block lane cut through from Manners Street to Dixon Street by Dr Fitzherbert to give access to his subdivisions of the acre. In Plate 2, the small building seen just above the chimneypots of the Custom House stands at about the spot, and may even be the 'log-house' of Charlotte Brontë's reference. Waring was in the heart, therefore, of the mercantile community such as it then was, and dealt in land, wool, cattle, clothing and piece goods, and general commodities of every kind. Even leeches appear now and then in his advertisements.

Of Mary's activities in 1845-6 no local evidence survives, but Waring was in Sydney early in 1846, so that she may have been left in charge during his absence. If so, this could well have been the 'toilsome task' to which Charlotte referred in September 1846. Waring returned in July on the *Levant,* having as fellow passenger his future father-in-law, Dr Frederick John Knox (*New Zealand Spectator,* 25 July 1846). In March 1847, Mary inserted a 'card' in the *Spectator* (March 12, 19, etc.) to this effect: 'Instructions on the Piano Forte, MISS TAYLOR, Herbert Street, Te Aro'.

About this time also, Mary built a house, which she let for 12/- a week. Waring acted as her agent, advertising in April 1848 'A five-roomed house, situate in Cuba Street, Te Aro.' When in 1854 the house fell vacant, Mary handled the transaction herself, inserting this advertisement in the *Wellington Independent* for 24 June: 'Miss Taylor advertises A Dwelling House Situate in Cuba-street, Te Aro. There is a good well of water and a pump. For particulars, apply Miss Taylor, corner of Cuba Street' (i.e., at her shop). By 1857, Mary's tenant in this house was Charles Augustus Vallance, who also dealt at her shop, as his journal reveals. One of her bills to him is reproduced in Plate 4.

Set about Wellington Town on all sides except Te Aro Flat are steep hills. When in June 1848 Mary climbed to the top of Mt Victoria to look for a ship to carry her letter to Yorkshire, it was to the shipping signal station (648 feet) that she clambered. Mt Victoria lies at the end of the eastward curve of the shoreline, where the beginning of its slope may be seen at the extreme left in Plate 2. Mary would have had to cross the Taranaki swamp as well as the creek that drained out from what is now the Basin Reserve, but there was a rough road, which would have presented no difficulties to a staunch moor-walker such as she was.

In these first years, Mary lodged in various households; sometimes she was with Waring in Herbert Street; sometimes in the Thorndon area with the recently widowed William Couper, whose daughter she had undertaken to instruct in music. Later, she lodged with Mrs Knox, during one of the Doctor's absences from home. The Knoxes lived in Willis Street, under the hill.[1]

On 14 February 1848 Waring Taylor married Mary Knox, aged twenty-one, his sister being one of those who signed the register. Mary Knox's father, one of the notable personalities of early Wellington, was not however the anatomist of the Edinburgh Medical School scandal, as Charlotte suspected. Knox the Anatomist was Dr *Robert* Knox; Waring's father-in-law was Dr Frederick John Knox, Robert's brother; he had however been Robert's collaborator in many anatomical investigations, including their famous study of the Blue Whale that washed onto the Scottish shore near Dunbar in 1831. Its skeleton still hangs in the Royal Scottish Museum, Edinburgh, 'prepared', as its label says, 'by Drs Robert and Frederick Knox.'

Some of the opprobrium that shadowed Dr Robert's life after the Burke and Hare murder trials undoubtedly came the way of Dr Frederick. This may be why, in July 1840, at the age of fifty, he sailed off to New Zealand as Official Surgeon on the New Zealand Company's emigrant ship *Martha Ridgway,* with his wife and five children. On arrival he was promptly appointed Librarian of the hopeful little Public Library established by the Company in a raupo whare at the foot of Charlotte Street (now Molesworth Street), not far from Barrett's Hotel. To this Library Knox soon added a Museum, and there resumed his lifelong interest in zoology, whales and fish being his special concern. A tentative list of his published work—including two books

[1] This and following information is derived from Mary's letters, and from newspapers and private journals of the time. See Stevens, 'Brother Fred and the Two Cultures: New Zealand's First Librarian', in *New Zealand Libraries,* October 1968.

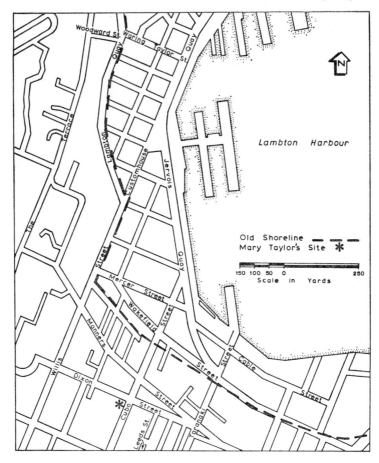

Lambton Harbour

Old Shoreline ▬ ▬ ▬
Mary Taylor's Site ✳

150 100 50 0   250
Scale in Yards

published in Scotland—numbers 56 items, mostly on New
Zealand topics. Neither Mary nor Ellen Taylor liked Dr
Knox, but Ellen's verdict that he was 'an idle fool' cannot
be allowed to stand. (See Stevens, in *New Zealand Libraries,* October 1968). The Public Library and Museum of
1840 did not flourish, however, and in 1842 Knox handed
over its contents to the Mechanics' Institute, which in its
turn had a chequered career.

Three of Dr Knox's daughters appear in Mary Taylor's
correspondence. Mary Knox married Waring Taylor in

February 1848; Margaret in September of the same year married William Couper; and a third daughter, not named, seemed to Mary to be likely to marry Captain W. B. Rhodes, one of Waring's business and political associates, and a leading citizen.

William Couper (1804-52), grazier and cattle dealer, was, according to E. J. Wakefield (*Adventure in New Zealand*, ed. of 1908, p. 246) 'an industrious Scotch carpenter, who had left a whaling ship some years before.' In 1839, Couper had bought some thousands of acres in the Porirua-Titahi Bay area to the north-west of Wellington, paying the Maori owners in blankets, muskets, tobacco, and cash to the value of £45. He built a house on his land in 1844, and ran cattle, but his claim was reduced to 600 acres by the Land Claims Commission of 1845. His estate was visited in March 1846 by Governor Grey, and in June 1848 by Thomas Arnold (*New Zealand Letters*, pp. 52-3). Arnold's description of Couper's 'ugly house and filthy homestead', and of his money-making 'shifts and speculations' confirms Mary's opinion of the man. Couper's first wife died in July 1847; soon after this he approached Mary 'to go and teach his daughter'. His 'interested civilities' may indeed have been the matrimonial feelers which the local gossips assumed that they were. He married Margaret Knox in September 1848, he being then forty-four and she twenty.

In October 1848, Wellington 'Town' suffered a severe earthquake, which shook down its structures all around Mary and her relations. Bethune's brick house on the Terrace cracked open, Captain Rhodes's buildings collapsed, as did the Ordnance Stores, the Wesleyan Chapel, and the Sturdee Street Military Hospital. Dr Fitzherbert's store was damaged, and the houses in Dixon Street were 'much shaken'.

Dr James Hansard's two-storied brick building in Manners Street was 'completely shattered'. But Waring Taylor's little colonial cottage in Herbert Street, in the midst of all these, survived with only the loss of its chimneys. He took the opportunity, as Mary relates, of moving the old building back on its section, and erecting instead on the frontage

a new combined house and store. Meanwhile he lived in a
small house nearby, where his first child, Ann, was born
in January 1849. Mary moved into the old cottage at the
back, and settled down to wait the necessary months for the
arrival of her cousin Ellen Taylor, who landed in August
that year.

The tale of the shop which the two women planned and
built is best left to Mary's own telling, but the following
account may be useful as background.

The cousins leased a subdivision of Town Acre 178, at
the south-western point of the intersection of Dixon and
Cuba Streets. It was only a couple of hundred yards away
from Waring's Herbert Street store, and about the same
distance from Captain Rhodes's wharf at the foot of Cuba
Street.

The building which they erected in 1850, and to which
Mary added in 1853-54, survived long enough to be photo-
graphed, while Mary left sketches of both the original
ground plan and the extended frontage view of 1854. See
pages 89 and 121, and Plate 5. The shop opened onto Cuba
Street, with the kitchen behind it on the longer Dixon Street
side. Because of its two storeys and gabled roof, the building can be picked out in the 1851 sketch of Te Aro shown in
Plate 3. This view looks northward across the Te Aro Flat;
Cuba Street, which at that time began only at Vivian Street
in the centre of the Flat, leads down past nothing in particular to the shoreline below Manners Street. As a measure
of the grandeur which Mary's small building represented in
1850, the following account is of interest. Charles R. Carter,
in his *Life and Recollections of a New Zealand Colonist*
(pp. 3-7) noted that in 1850 Wellington was a 'clean and
agreeable, but primitive town', in which 'the houses were
nearly all built of wood, and mostly one storey in height
. . . . in a style of genuine simplicity—a long, narrow, but
very large box: the sides fronting the streets were about 8
feet in height and 20 to 24 feet in length: they had a door
in the middle, and a window about 5 ft by 3 ft on each side
of the door . . . these truly convenient and comfortable
colonial cottages . . . being generally painted white, looked

clean, neat, and fresh.' Clearly 'Miss Taylor's Shop', two storeys in height and on a ground plan of 28 by 26 feet, was an ambitious venture.

Ellen Taylor died in December 1851, and Mary thereafter carried on alone for some years. By 1853, 'Miss Taylor, Cuba Street' was being listed in the *Wellington and Southern Province Almanac* as one of the 'Principal Stores'. She was obviously prospering. She enlarged the shop, and took on an assistant, Miss M. Smith. By this time, building had progressed further up Cuba Street. Mary's first neighbour, the edge of whose house can be seen on the left of the photograph in Plate 5, was a plumber, David Kinniburgh, a staunch member of the Church of Scotland. His sister later became the owner of the sewing machine which Mary imported, the first, it is said, in the settlement. (Ward, pp. 218, 221, 304, 392.) Further up Cuba Street Dr Logan came to live, one of Mary's 'few intelligent friends'. Both the Kinniburgh and Logan households must have been among those to which Mary went, as she told Ellen Nussey, for 'gossip with a neighbour' and some '*real talk*' after she had shut up the shop at night.

We have two personal recollections of Mary Taylor in her later Wellington years. In 1926 the correspondent 'Old Hand' in the *New Zealand Free Lance* (14 July) wrote 'There cannot be many persons living who remember [Miss Taylor's shop] or the lady herself . . . . As a child, I remember purchasing marbles and jew's harps there. The shop then, as at present, was very well known, and very well patronised in the early days.' Another memory, recorded by 'S.F.D.' in the *Dominion* (4 December 1937) is of Mary's pony: 'I remember her as she used to ride out to the Hutt [Valley] to visit my grandparents . . . Miss Taylor and my aunt had many pleasant jaunts together, and I can remember Miss Taylor putting me up on her pony and leading me round the paddock. She called him "Korey", it must have been just before she left for England.'

At her departure in May 1859 Mary invested some £400 of her capital in two blocks of land, one in Abel Smith Street and one in Ghuznee Street. The latter, Town Acre

181, is the site of the present Te Aro Post Office; an access street into it was cut, appropriately named Leeds Street.

The shop was taken over by Miss Smith and her sister, who continued in the business until 1866. In that year, from April to September, they advertised 'Clearing Sale of Drapery, Silk, Mercery, Haberdashery, etc' in the *Wellington Independent*. The business was then bought by a Scots settler of the same name, though no relation, James Smith. He made much of his purchase as being an 'OLD ESTABLISHED Drapery Business . . . so long and successfully conducted' (*Wellington Independent,* 27 September 1866, etc.) He closed for alterations to the interior, and reopened on 4 October 1866, assisted by his wife Annie and one other. He named the shop Te Aro House, and took its photograph to mark the occasion. This is reproduced in Plate 5; it will be noted that the outline of the facade is still that which Mary sketched in 1854 (see p. 121), and that Smith has boarded up the window on the Dixon Street side.

Just over one hundred years have passed since then. In 1885 the little gabled building which Ellen Taylor had worried over met the fate she had feared for it, and was destroyed by fire. James Smith rebuilt on the same site. At the turn of the century the firm moved to the other corner of Dixon Street, and in 1920 moved again, to its present situation at the corner of Manners Street and Cuba Street. Here, in Mary Taylor's day, Bethune and Hunter's cattle yards looked across the street to the ground behind Captain Rhodes's residence. Today 'James Smith's Corner' is in the commercial heart of the City, and Mary's 28 by 26 feet shop of 1850 with boards overlapping and a shingle roof— 'by far the best house on our acre—' has developed into a store covering three acres and employing over 500 assistants. On Mary's original corner, Te Aro House stood until the 1930s; the site is now occupied by Woolworth's.

Thus, though Mary's shop was never 'large', as Mrs Gaskell imagined (Gaskell, *Letters* no. 256), she tasted success in New Zealand. She built a house and a business, and maintained herself 'free of debt and dependence', knowing as she did so those 'blessings of change and activity'

which fate had largely denied to her friend Charlotte
Brontë, as to many other English gentlewomen of that time.
Her experience strengthened the conviction which she had
expressed to Charlotte long before, and which she put into
print in her articles and her novel, that a woman's first duty,
like a man's, is to earn a living (*Miss Miles*, pp. 281, 423-5,
etc, and the articles, passim).

And so we come to the first survivor of Mary's correspondence from New Zealand. It is postmarked Wellington
24 July 1848, and Charlotte received it on 14 December.

LETTER 16

*Mary Taylor to Charlotte Brontë, June to 24 July 1848,
WS no. 382.*[1]

(a)

Dear Charlotte

About a month since I received and read *Jane Eyre*. It
seemed to me incredible that you had actually written a
book. Such events did not happen while I was in England. I
begin to believe in your existence much as I do in Mr Roch-
ester's. In a believing mood I don't doubt either of them.
After I had read /it/ I went on to the top of Mt. Victoria
and looked for a ship to carry a letter to you. There was a
little thing with one mast, and also H.M.S. *Fly*,[2] and nothing
else. If a cattle vessel came from Sydney she would probably
return in a few days and would take a mail, but we have had
east wind for a month and nothing can come in. — /July 1/

---

[1] The MS. of (a) is in the Pierpont Morgan Library, New York,
and that of (b) in the Berg Collection, New York Public Library.
The postmarks on (a) include 'Wellington New Zealand Jy
24, 1848', 'Keighley De 14, 1848' and 'Bradford Yorks De 14,
1848'. WS no. 382 prints the text as one letter, which it clearly is.

[2] H.M.S. *Fly*, sloop, 18 guns, had been in Wellington since April.
She sailed for Akaroa, in the South Island, on 4 June, returning
on 16 June, either of which days may therefore be the date of
Mary's climb up the signal station on Mt Victoria (Oliver).

The Harlequin has just come from Otago[3] and is to sail for
Singapore *when the wind changes* and by that route (which
I hope to take myself sometime) I send you this. Much good
may it do you.

✗ ⎰   Your novel surprised me by being so perfect as a work of
  ⎱ art. I expected something more changeable and unfinished.
You have polished to some purpose. If I were to do so I
should get tired and weary every one else in about two
pages. No sign of this weariness is in your book—you must
have had abundance, having kept it all to yourself!

You are very different from me in having no doctrine to
preach. It is impossible to squeeze a moral out of your production. Has the world gone so well with you that you have
no protest to make against its absurdities? Did you never
sneer or declaim in your first sketches? I will scold you well
when I see you.—I don't believe in Mr Rivers. There are no
good men of the Brocklehurst species. A missionary[4] either
goes into his office for a piece of bread, or he goes from
enthusiasm, and that is both too good and too bad a quality
for St. John. It's a bit of your absurd charity to believe in
such a man. You have done wisely in choosing to imagine a
high class of readers. You never stop to explain or defend
anything and never seem bothered with the idea—if Mrs
Fairfax[5] or any other well intentioned fool gets hold of this
what will she think? And yet you know the world is made
up of such, and worse. Once more, how have you written
through 3 vols. without declaring war to the knife against a

---

[3] The *Harlequin* arrived on 29 June from Sydney via Otago, and
sailed again on 14 July.

[4] Mary ended with 'mission-' at the bottom of the recto of the
first page ; leaving its verso blank, she then wrote on with '-ary'
on the recto of the second page. Finishing this at 'think of you',
she realized that she had missed 'one side of the paper', and went
back to write on the verso of the first page, ending it with 'perhaps make a'. The passage from 'better bargain' to 'mode of
living' is written on the verso of the second leaf, around the centre
panel on which the address is written.

[5] The housekeeper at Thornfield in *Jane Eyre ;* the name is common
in Yorkshire. CB may have had Miss Wooler in mind in drawing
the portrait of Mrs Fairfax.

few dozen absurd do[ct]rines each of which is supported by
"a large and respectable class of readers"? Emily seems
to have had such a class in her eye when she wrote that
strange thing Wuthering Heights. Ann too stops repeatedly
to preach commonplace truths. She has had a still lower
class in her mind's eye. Emily seems to have followed th[e
b]ookseller's advice. As to the price you got it [was] certainly Jewish.⁶ But what could the people do? If they had
asked you to fix it, do you know yourself how many cyphers
your sum would have had? And how should they know
better? And if they did, that's the knowledge they get their
living by. If I were in your place the idea of being bound
in the sale of 2! more would prevent from ever writing
again. Yet you are probably now busy with another. It is
curious to me to see among the old letters one from A.
Sarah⁷ sending a *copy of* a *whole article* on the currency
question written by Fonblanque!⁸ I exceedingly regret having
burnt your letters in a fit of caution, and I've forgotten all
the names. Was the reader Albert Smith?⁹ What do they
all think of you? I perceive I've betrayed my habit of writing only on one side of the paper. Go on to the next page.

I mention the book to no one and hear no opinions. I
lend it a good deal because it's a novel and it's *as good as
another!* They say "it makes them cry." They are not literary enough to give an opinion. If ever I hear one I'll embalm
it for you.

As to my own affair I have written 100 pages and lately

⁶ CB received £500 for *Jane Eyre* (WS II, p. 236).

⁷ Sarah Taylor, Mary's aunt.

⁸ Albany Fonblanque (1793-1872), editor of the *Examiner* 1830-47,
reviewed *Jane Eyre* on 27 November 1847. CB valued his opinion:
'I am willing to be judged by the *Examiner*. Fonblanque has
power, he has discernment' (WS no. 488). She placed an extract
from his review at the head of a group of criticisms appended to
the 3rd edition of *Jane Eyre*, published in April 1848. Presumably
she had mentioned his opinions to Mary.

⁹ William Smith Williams was the reader of the MS. of *Jane Eyre ;*
for his reaction to it, see Gérin, pp. 337-41. Albert Smith (1816-
60) was a popular journalist.

50 more.[10] It's no use writing faster. I get so disgusted I can do nothing. I have sent 3 or 4 things to Joe for Tait.[11] Troup (Ed.) never acknowledges them though he promised either to pay or send them back. Joe sent one to Chambers[12] who thought it unsuitable in which I agree with them.

I think I told you I built a house.[13] I get 12/- a week for it. Moreover in accordance with a late letter of John's I borrow money from him and Joe and buy cattle with it.[14] I have already spent £100 or so and intend to buy some more as soon as War. [i.e., Waring] can pay me the money. —perhaps as much *by degrees* as £400, or £500. As I only pay 5 per Ct. interest I expect [to] profit much by this. viz. about 30 per Ct. a year—perhaps 40 or 50. Thus if I borrow £500 in two years' time (I cannot have it quicker) I shall perhaps make £250 to £300. I am pretty certain of being able to pay principal and interest. If I could command £300 and £50 a year afterwards I would *"hallack"*[15] about N.Z. for a twelvemonth then go home by way of India and write my travels which would prepare the way for my novel. With the benefit of your experience I should perhaps make a better bargain than you. I am most afraid of my health. Not that I shd die but perhaps sink into state of *betweenity,* neither well nor ill, in which I shd observe nothing and be very miserable besides.—My life here is not disagreeable. I have a great resource in the piano, and a little employment in teaching.[16] Then I go in to Mrs Taylor's and astonish the

10 Mary must be referring to her novel, *Miss Miles,* not published until 1890.

11 *Tait's Edinburgh Magazine,* edited by George Troup (1821-79).

12 *Chambers's Edinburgh Journal.*

13 Waring Taylor advertised this house for his sister in April 1848 (*New Zealand Spectator*): 'A five-roomed house, situate in Cuba St., Te Aro.'

14 In her will Mary left £40 a year to her brother John. John, Joseph and Waring all helped Mary, but her eldest brother Joshua seems not to have given aid.

15 i.e., 'hallock', Yorkshire dialect word meaning to idle, to loiter.

16 The *New Zealand Spectator* for 13 March 1847 carried this advertisement: 'Instruction on the Piano Forte, MISS TAYLOR, Herbert St., Te Aro.'

poor girl with calling her favorite parson a *spoon*.[17] She
/thinks/ I am astonishingly learned but rather wicked, and
tries hard to persuade me to go to chapel, though I tell her
I only go for amusement. She would have sense but for her
wretched health which is getting rapidly worse from her
irrational mode of living.[18]

(*b*)

I can hardly explain to you the queer feeling of living as I
do in 2 places at once. One world containing books England
and all the people with whom I can exchange an idea; the
other all that I actually see and hear and speak to. The sep-
aration is as complete as between the things in a picture and
the things in the room. The puzzle is that both move and
act, and [I] must say my say as one of each. The result is
that one world at least must think me crazy. I am just now
in a sad mess. A drover who has got rich with cattle dealing
wanted me to go and teach his daughter.[19] As the man is a
widower I astonished *this* world when I accepted the proposal, and still more because I asked too high a price (£70)
a year. Now that I have begun the same people can't conceive why I don't go on and marry the man at once which
they imagine must have been my original intention. For my
part I shall possibly astonish them a little more for I feel a
great inclination to make use of his interested civilities to
visit his daughter and see the district of Porirua.

If [I] had a little more money and could afford a horse

17 Mrs Waring Taylor was a member of the Congregational Church
founded by Jonas Woodward in 1842. At that time services were
held in the Mechanics' Institute room at the junction of Charlotte
Street and Lambton Quay, where her father Dr Knox had conducted his Library in 1841. By 1845 Woodward's congregation
numbered '64 souls'. Woodward was employed as an accountant
by the firm of Bethune and Hunter, and became a leader in the
settlement in educational and religious matters (Ward). In her
next sentence Mary at first wrote 'church', then crossed it out in
favour of 'chapel'.

18 There are five postmarks on the address panel here, including
'Wellington New Zealand Jy 24, 1848' and 'Keighley De 14,
1848'.

19 William Couper (1804-52), see the Introduction to Part III.

(she rides) I certainly would. But I can see nothing til' I get a horse, which I shall have if I am lucky in 2 or 3 years.

I have just made acquaintance with Dr and Mrs Logan.[20] He is a retired navy doctor and has more general knowledge than any one I have talked to here. For instance he had heard of Phillippe Egalité[21]—of a camera obscura; of the resemblance the English language has to the German etc etc. Mrs Taylor Miss Knox[22] and Mrs Logan sat in mute admiration while we mentioned these things, being employed in the meantime in making a patchwork quilt. Did you never notice that the women of the *middle classes* are generally too ignorant to talk to?, and that you are thrown entirely on the men for conversation? There is no such feminine inferiority in the lower. The women go hand in hand with the men in the degree of cultivation they are able to reach. I can talk very well to a joiner's wife, but seldom to a merchant's.

I must now tell you the fate of your cow.[23] The creature gave so little milk that she is doomed to be fatted and killed. In about 2 months she will fetch perhaps £15 with which I

[20] Dr Francis H. Logan (1784-1862), R.N. He entered the Navy in 1811, and later served in the convict ships *Champion* (1827), *Fanny* (1832-33), *Royal Sovereign* (1835-36) and *Mangles* (1837), all on voyages to Sydney. In September 1837 he returned to England as a passenger on the *John Barry,* paying a visit on the way to northern New Zealand. He was so impressed by what he saw that on return to Glasgow in 1839 he joined the New Zealand Company's West of Scotland Committee and became an advocate of colonization. On 30 October 1839 he sailed from the Clyde with his wife and young son as Official Surgeon on the Company's emigrant ship *Bengal Merchant.* Its departure was marked by a public banquet, at which Dr Logan spoke, though apparently he was inaudible. The *Glasgow Argus* reported him as a 'hale old veteran, whose general intelligence and experience in the country to which he is bound, may be of essential service to his fellow emigrants' (31 October 1839).

[21] Louis Phillippe Joseph, duc d'Orleans (1747-93), French revolutionary.

[22] Margaret Knox, sister of Mrs Waring Taylor.

[23] cf Charlotte's letter to Miss Wooler, 28 August 1848. WS surmise that this beast was bought with the £10 which Charlotte sent to Mary, as recorded in Mary's letter to Mrs Gaskell, in Appendix B (extract 6 of the second letter).

shall buy 3 heifers. Thus you have the chance of getting a calf *sometime*. My own thrive well and possibly I [shall] have a calf myself. Before this reaches England I shall have 3 or 4.

It's a pity you don't live in this world that I might entertain you about the price of meat. Do you know I bought 6 heifers the other day for £23? and now it is turned so cold I expect to hear one half of them are dead. One man bought 20 sheep for £8 and they are all dead but 1. Another bought £1.50[24] and has 40 left; and people have begun to drive cattle through a valley into the Wairau plains[25] and thence across the Straits to Wellington. etc etc. This is the only legitimate subject of conversation we have the rest is gos[sip] concerning our superiors in station who don't know us in the road, but it is astonishing how well we know all their private affairs, making allowance always for the distortion in our own organs of vision.

I have now told you everything I can think of except that the cat's on the table and that I'm going to borrow a new book to read. No less than an account of all the systems of philosophy of modern Europe.[26] I have lately met with a wonder a man who thinks Jane Eyre would have done better [to] marry Mr Rivers! he gives no reasons—such people never do.

Mary Taylor

July 24 1848

Letter 16 crossed with Charlotte's letter of 4 September, with its account of the visit to London (see Appendix E). On 10 December, Charlotte complained to Ellen Nussey that it was 'very long indeed' since she had heard from Mary, adding 'Nor was I aware that Ellen Taylor was to go to New Zealand'. (This last phrase, omitted in WS no. 409, is in

---

[24] Thus in MS.

[25] Wairau Valley, Marlborough.

[26] Probably John Daniel Morell's *Historical and Critical View of the Speculative Philosophy of Europe in the Nineteenth Century.* 2 vols. London, 1846. A second edition appeared in 1847.

the MS. at the Amy Lowell Collection, Harvard.) Charlotte was, of course, preoccupied at the time with Emily's mortal illness, following so soon upon the death of Branwell. Mary's *Jane Eyre* budget arrived four days later, only five days before Emily died. By 22 January 1849 Charlotte still had not written to either Mary or Ellen Taylor, feeling that she had 'nothing but dreary news to write and preferred that others should tell her—' (WS no. 418).

Mary wrote again on 9 February 1849, this time to Ellen Nussey.

LETTER 17

Mary Taylor to Ellen Nussey, 9 February 1849, WS no. 422; text from MS. in Berg Collection, New York Public Library. No postmark.

Dear Ellen,

You will think it ridiculous in me to begin to try to persuade you to come out to N.Z. after all. Still more when I know as little of your circumstances as I do just now. But you must not laugh at me for this is the serious purpose of my letter. I hear fm C. Brontë that you are staying in Sussex. What in the world are you doing there?[1] Getting your living in any way? not at all—you are only wishing to do. Wishing for something to turn up that wd enable you to work for yourself instead of for other people and that no one shd know that you were working. Now no such thing exists. There are no means for a woman to live in England but by teaching, sewing or washing. The last is the best. The best paid the least unhealthy and the most free. But it is not paid well enough to live by. Moreover it is impossible for any one not born to this position to take it up afterwards. I don't know why but it is. You might as well ask

---

[1] Ellen Nussey stayed in Sussex with the Gorham family at West Wittering, near Chichester, in July and August 1848. The visit is discussed in CB's letters of 26 June, 28 July, 18 and 28 August (WS nos. 379, 383, 387, 388). See also p. 112.

why one can't move when they have the nightmare, when they know very well—the stupid things! that they need only just move to send the horror away. If you do it at all it will be by making a desperate plunge, and you will come up in another world. The new world will be no Paradise but still much better than the nightmare. Am I not right in all this? and dont you know it very well? Or am I shooting in the dark? I must say I judge ra[ther] by my own history than fm any actuall[2] knowledge of yours. Still you yourself must judge for no one else can. What in the world keeps you? Try and persuade some of your twenty brothers[3] to fit you out for N. Zealand. You could get your living here at any of the trades I have mentioned which you wd only d ⟨··⟩ of in England. As to "society" position in the world you must have found by this time it is all my eye seeking society without the means to enjoy it. Why not come here then? and be happy.

We have had occurences[4] here nearly as startling as those in Europe.[5] Lots of earthquakes—till they are quite common place. This is small inducement but what do you think of our sending back a subscription raised in Auckland for us because we actually had no destitute to give it to.[6] Are n't we thriving?

[2] Thus in MS.

[3] There were nine boys and four girls in Ellen's family.

[4] Thus in MS.

[5] 1848 was a year of renewed revolution in Europe. A severe earthquake struck Wellington on 16 October. See Introduction to Part III.

[6] Auckland churchmen and citizens convened a public meeting to raise funds for Earthquake Relief (*The New-Zealander*, 18 November). Accompanied by expressions of sympathy, a sum of £500 reached Wellington in mid-November, with the promise of more. At a Public Meeting on 30 November, Wellington citizens expressed their 'just appreciation', but voted to return the money with 'warmest thanks', because Aucklanders had been 'under an exaggerated impression of the losses' (*New Zealand Spectator*, 29 November, 2 December 1848). The episode is typical of the rivalry existing, then as now, between Auckland and Wellington.

The Maories are quiet and we begin to wish for another disturbance for fear the troops should leave the country.[7]

We have just been to the anniversary races[8] and amused ourselves pretty well and got heartily tired It did us a deal of good however. We means Mrs Knox, all the children, and her married daughter Mrs Couper, her husband and step-daughter.[9] Miss Couper is nearly as old as her new Mama, and they are both so girlish that they agree very well together. Mr Couper himself is coarse, ugly, selfish, ignorant cunning and dishonest and all this in the highest degree; however this only concerns his wife. To me he is very civil because he has the idea that he gets his daughter taught music very cheap when he gives me board and lodging for teaching her, *when she has time* which is only half an hour now and then. To be sure I pass here for a monkey who has seen the world and people receive me well on that account. I wonder what good it does them to have the acquaintance of a person that speaks French? They don't want to learn it.

I once thought of delaying this letter until Ellen Taylor came, but I am in doubt as to whether she is on the way or not and if she comes I shall not have as much time for writing as I have just now. She will be quite an acquisition to me if she comes. I speak of it so much that the children rouse me

[7] Trouble with the Maori people of the area was quelled by Governor Grey in 1846.

[8] Races held on Monday 22 January 1849, the ninth Anniversary of the arrival of the first body of Company settlers in the *Aurora,* 1840. Entertainments were various, and included water sports and athletics. The races were held at Burnham Water Course, a track made by draining the lake on J. C. Crawford's estate at Miramar. Thomas Arnold also described these races: 'everyone flocked, booths were put up, flags were flying, all the people were in holiday garb' (*New Zealand Letters,* pp. 32-4). The day is still observed as a Provincial holiday.

[9] Mrs Knox (née Margaret Russell), Waring Taylor's mother-in-law, and her younger children. (Five children came with them from Scotland in 1840, a daughter was born in 1841, and a son, who did not survive, in 1847). Margaret Knox, aged twenty, had married William Couper, aged forty-four, four months previously, in September 1848. See Introduction to Part III.

in the morning with "Miss Taylor here are your cousins come!"[10]

Mrs Taylor got a little daughter a month ago.[11] Waring is going to build a new house. As the chimneys of the present one were entirely shaken down by the earthquake it is just ready for moving back. He will put 2 new rooms in front 2 stories high. One will be a store and one a parlour. Two fiths[12] if not half the houses in Wellington were shaken down by the earthquake and the town is vastly improved in consequence. Almost every body is building. We think nothing of what we have lost because no one was ruined. At least only one man whose house was entirely destroyed. He was a Doctor and got such a fright he resolved to go to Sydney. The vessel he was in was wrecked just outside Wellington harbour and he brought his family back again to Wellington having lost everything on the wreck. Fortunately a box was picked up with his money in and he took his passage for Sydney as soon as possible. He is now on his way to England.[13]

I have just written an account of my present condition and prospects 3 times over. I therefore recommend you to ask C. Brontë for an abstract of it, for it is so dull telling the same tale so often. I should perhaps be inventing something for a change if I were to write all the history over again.

You have never followed the advice I sent you to send

[10] Ellen Taylor and William Henry Taylor sailed on the *Jane Catherine* on 10 February 1849, and arrived at Wellington on 16 August.

[11] Ann, b. 23 December 1848, died 14 December 1857.

[12] Thus in MS.

[13] The *Subraon,* barque, 510 tons, leaving Wellington on 26 October 1848, tried to negotiate the inner passage at Barrett's Reef at the harbour entrance, but went onto the rocks. Captain Oliver of H.M.S. *Fly* gave assistance, and all the passengers were safely transferred ashore. The Doctor of Mary's reference was James T. Hansard, who had arrived in Wellington in the *New York Packet* from London in 1843, and lived in a two-storied brick building in Manners St. His house was 'completely shattered' (*New Zealand Spectator,* 28 October and 4 November 1848 ; Ingram ; Ward).

something out to sell. When I received your parcel of collars I thought they were for sale and as they were the height of the fashion here I shd have sold them very well. As it is I wear them and get envied. The thick one with lace round I sometimes ride in and tell every one that I have two friends in England wearing the same. I wish I could say I had them here. You will think my persuasions for you to come are like those of the fox who had lost his tail. They are certainly selfish but not entirely so. Wherever you are always believe me

    your sincere friend Mary Taylor

Wellington Feb 9 1849

  Meanwhile in Yorkshire Charlotte told Ellen on 16 February 1849: 'Last Sunday I got a short note from Ellen Taylor written in London—they had been in town waiting for the vessel to sail a fortnight—they expected to be off that day—Joe Taylor had left them a week ago—she and Harry were quite alone—poor things!' (WS no. 423). They sailed on the *Jane Catherine* on 10 February 1849, and arrived at Wellington on 16 August.

  In May 1849, Mary's letter after the earthquake of October 1848 reached her friends. 'Thank God she was safe up to that time' wrote Charlotte (WS no. 441).

  In July, Charlotte told Ellen Nussey of another long letter: 'interesting but sad—because it contained many allusions to those who are in this world no more'. (Anne Brontë had died on 28 May). Mary's letter had commented on the 'lamentable nature' of Ellen Nussey's 'unoccupied life', and spoke of her own health as being excellent (WS no. 453; the MS. in Brontë Parsonage Museum is mistakenly dated 1848).

  In October arrived Mary's reply to the long description of Charlotte and Anne's visit to London in July 1848.

LETTER 18

Mary Taylor to Charlotte Brontë, 10 April 1849, WS no. 436; text from MS. in Brontë Parsonage Museum, Haworth.[1]

Dear Charlotte

I've been delighted to receive a very interesting letter from you with an account of your pop visit to London etc. I believe I have tacked this acknowledgement to the tail of my last letter to you but since then it has dawned on my comprehension that you are becoming a very important personage in this little world and therefore d'yer see? I must write again to you. I wish you would give me some account of Newby, and what the man said when confronted with the real Ellis Bell.[2] By the way having got your secret will he keep it? And how do you contrive to get your letters under the address of Mr Bell? The whole scheme must be particularly interesting to hear about, if I could only talk to you for half a day. When do you intend to tell the good people about you?

I am now hard at work expecting Ellen Taylor. She may possibly be here in two months. In the mean time I have left Couper's and am at present living with the Knoxes. Now the old Dr came home a few days ago and will neither do any work nor follow his profession but will live on his wife; who maintains herself and the children principally with my lodging money and a little sewing and some charity fm Waring and Couper. Now the Dr's arrival has determined me to flit; so I have ordered a chimney to Waring's old house and shall make myself comfortable there. This house has been moved back fm the road and a new one is building in front of it to be finished in 2 mos [months]. Then the back cottage where

[1] The address panel is annotated 'Hunsworth 27 Oct. 1849 via Sydney', but there is no postmark.

[2] Thomas Cautley Newby, of Mortimer St, Cavendish Square, had published *Wuthering Heights* by 'Ellis Bell' and *Agnes Grey* by 'Acton Bell' in December 1847. But it was Anne ('Acton'), not Emily, who accompanied Charlotte to London. Charlotte's letter is in Appendix E.

Waring now lives will be whieled[3] on to a neighbour's
ground; said neighbour paying £10 for it. I once thought of
writing to you some of the dozens of schemes I have for E.T.
but as the choice depends on her I think I may as well wait
and tell you the one she chooses. The 2 most reasonable are,
keeping a school and keeping a shop. The last is decidedly
the most healthy, but the most difficult of accomplishment.

I have written an account of the earthquakes for Chambers[4] and intend (now dont remind me of this a year hence,
because "la femme proposes") to write some more. The next
to be "Physiognomy of the town of Wellington". What else
I shall do I don't know. I find the writing faculty does not
in the least depend on the leisure I have; much more on the
active work I have to do. I write at my novel a little and
think of my other book. What this will turn out God only
knows. It is not and never can be forgotten. It is my child,
my baby and I *assure you* such a wonder as never was. I
intend him when full grown to revolutionize society and
faire époque in history.[5]

In the meantime I'm doing a collar in crochet work.

Pag.   Wellington April 10 1849

In January 1850 more New Zealand mail arrived, and
Charlotte wrote to Ellen at once: 'Herewith are enclosed
three letters for your perusal—the first from Mary Taylor—
which you are to read immediately (so the order runs) and
return direct to Joe. You are *not to send it* to Mrs Burnley'
(WS no. 521; text from MS. in Berg Collection, New York
Public Library). This was Mrs Thomas Burnley, of Pollard
House, neighbour to the Red House, Gomersal, who is mentioned in Letter 11. On 28 January, Charlotte added 'Mary

---

[3] Thus in MS.

[4] *Chambers's Edinburgh Journal.* Mary's account was not published,
perhaps because an editorial compilation derived from H. S.
Chapman's article in the *Westminster Review* for July 1849 was
printed on 22 September 1849.

[5] Possibly this 'other book' is the material on the position of women
in Mary's articles?

Taylor seems in good health and spirits and in the way of doing well' (WS no. 522).

Then came two full long budgets of news, sent off from Wellington in April 1850.

LETTER 19

Mary Taylor to Charlotte Brontë, 5 April 1850, WS no. 542; text from MS. in Miriam Lutcher Stark Library, University of Texas. No postmark.

Dear Charlotte

About a week since I received your last melancholy letter with the account of Ann's death and yr utter indifference to everything, even to the success of your last book.[1] Though you do not say this it is pre[tty] plain to be seen from the style of your letter. It seems to me hard indeed that you who would succeed better than anyone in making friends and keeping them should be condemned to solitude from you[r] poverty. To no one would money bring more happiness, for no one would use it better than you would.—For me with my headlong selfindulgent habits I am perhaps better without it, but I am convinced it would give you great and noble pleasures. Look out then for success in writing. You ought to care as much for that as you do for going to Heaven. Though the advantages of being employ[ed] appear to you now the best part of the business you will soon plea[se] God have other enjoyments from your success. Railway shares wil[l] rise,[2] your books will sell and you will acquire influence and power and then most certainly you will find some-

---

[1] Anne Brontë died in May 1849. Charlotte had begun *Shirley* in 1847, laid it aside at Emily's death in October 1848, resumed it during Anne's illness, and finished it for the publication date of 26 October 1849.

[2] Railway shares, in which Charlotte had invested after consulting Miss Wooler in 1845-46 (WS nos. 196 and 224). Values soon collapsed, causing the 'ruin that has now fallen upon thousands' (*Fraser's Magazine*, June 1849, pp. 607-18).

thing to use it in which will interest you and make you exert yourself.

What you say of Joe agrees with the melancholy account of him both in his own letters and other people's. I cannot give advic[e] or propose a remedy. All seems to depend on himself and he—like all other people with his disease, is so powerless! His passion for marryin[g] seems just to have come because it is the only thing serious enough to excite him—if that were done what would there be left? You[r] endeavour to persuade him to repose and quiet is certainly the best that could be made—may you succeed as you deserve! You will certainly do yourself good, tho it will be to both sides a melancholy meeting.[3]

My own concerns have advanced rapidly. As much in this last 6 months as in th[e] 4 years before. Ellen has come out with just the same wish to earn her living as I have and just the same objection to sedentary empl[oy]ment. We both enter heart and soul into the project of keeping a shop and actually hope to make £300 or £400 a year by it. John and Joe have helped her and me both with gifts and loans so that we begin with as large a capital as probably any in Wellington. We hope to have together fm £600 to £800. Our first step was to take some land (a st. corner) and build a house 28 ft by 26.[4] This is just in the heart of the town (*as laid out*)

---

[3] Joseph Taylor's eccentric behaviour and ill-health were constantly under discussion in Charlotte's letters. She had once admired him, but became after 1845 increasingly puzzled by his materialistic outlook and range of flirtations. For a time in 1843 he seemed interested in Ellen Nussey (WS nos. 150, 151) ; then he fluttered round Isabel Nussey, Ellen's second cousin (WS nos. 197, 215, 219, etc) ; in August 1846 he was wavering in various directions (WS no. 265) ; and by November 1849 Charlotte was noting with amusement his attraction to Amelia Ringrose, who had been engaged to George Nussey, Ellen's brother, before his mental decline (WS no. 487). After further vacillations, in the course of which he sought Charlotte's advice (WS nos. 492 and 548), he finally decided on Amelia, and married her in September 1850. But his domestic affairs continued to occupy the minds of his friends and relations. He died of liver disease on 23 March 1857.

[4] For details, see Introduction to Part III.

nevertheless unti[l] our house was built you could not see a st. at all, and the usual cart-road goes just thro the middle of it. Since we leased our bit 3 more people have taken the rest and one man has built a house and got into it.

It is just now blowing a cold South easter. I am sitting up stairs in a room with 2 windows looking into the east, by a glowing fire. In one room behind are 6 pieces paper hangings to be hung tomorrow; it is our bed room. In the other some crockery to be sold—when the house is finished. One back room down-stairs is top full of groceries, to be sold when the house is finished but alas in each of the other 2 rooms is a carpenter's bench, and there are 6 doors ways[5] wanting doors. Our new house [de]lights us with its roomy comfort and now let me tell you what roomy comf[ort] is. First understand it is made of boards overlapping, nailed to upright posts. Our uprights are $2\frac{1}{2}$ inches by 3. and the level piece at the bottom is blue gum a very hard heavy lasting wood fm Hobart town. Inside the house is lined with boards —but without overlapping. In the shop and kitchen these boards are planed and grooved together, in our bedroom they will be stretched with calico and papered and for the present the other 3 ro[oms] will be unfinished.[6] The rooms upstairs are only 2 ft high at the eaves. The best is 19 ft by 12. We think it handsome. —Now for what we are to do. First remember we have by far the best house on our acre and the best but one in our 2 streets. The shop will be *among* the first in [the] town and the situation too. I can scarcely tell you how I have learnt something of most of the people whom I shall have to buy of. Waring has dealt with them and I have lived in the same small town with them these 4 or 5 years. I know too the extent to which Waring sells on credit and how glad my [many] of these people would be to sell for money. Of

---

[5] Thus in MS.

[6] This sketch should be compared with the photograph reproduced in Plate 5, in which the '2 windows looking to the east' can be seen. The photograph was taken in 1866, looking westward across Cuba Street. The original structure which Mary is describing in this letter is the gabled half on the right.

most things too I know pretty well the prices I can get for them and what I ought to give. Waring gives m[e] his opinion too and many things we can get fm him and know the prices at home too.—Is this interesting? Well if it isn't here's some gossip. We have got a mechanic's institute and as it is the only place of (respectable) amusement in the town we encourage it with all our hearts—we encourage everything abt it but the objects it was instituted for.[7] One of these not-objects is dancing. So we (?) are going to open the new Hall wi[th] a dance by and by one half the member's sulking at it and the other half jus[t] carrying their point by dint of cunning. My share of the business is to find young ladies for these young gentlemen—of course the dancers are all young and I hope to get 6 or 7 who will be glad to avail themselves of the bachelors tickets. I cannot tell you with what zeal I labour to spite the "uneasy virtues" that are always saying something against "promiscuous dancing"—what a phrase. With many of them the objec[tion] is not to the character of the company but to their station. Of cour[se] *we* think our character much above our station and don't approve of being s[o] slighted. Besides we have and can have a pretty even number of ladies and gentlem[en] which is not easy to get any where else. So we crow over them and *won't* have them—as we don't want them. I have got into all this heap of social trickery since Ellen came, never having troubled

[7] The Mechanics' Institute had been first launched in May 1842, with a lecture given by Jonas Woodward (Mrs Taylor's 'favourite parson'). After a lapse, it revived again in 1848. Waring Taylor was on the Committee in 1849. In April 1850, at the time of this letter, the Institute, now entitled the Wellington Athenaeum and Mechanics' Institute, moved into its own hall in Lambton Quay. It was opened on Thursday 11 April, when Mr Justice H. S. Chapman made the official speech, 'long and elaborate', noted the *New Zealand Spectator* on 13 April. Chapman justified, by reference to English example, Wellington citizens' 'extension of their original plan, by which other classes besides mechanics were let in, and . . . the recreations of music and dancing [allowed]—converting them into places of agreeable relaxation to which the female portion of the families were admitted'. The platform was decorated, and the band of the 65th Regiment played. Double tickets cost 4/-, 'bachelors' tickets' 2/6.

my head before abt the comparative numbers of young ladies and young gentlemen.[8] To Ellen it is quite new to be of such importance by the mere fact of her femininity. She thot [thought] she was coming wofully down in the world when sh[e] came out and finds herself better received than ever she was in her life before. And the class are not *in education* inferior though they are in money. They are decent well to do people. 1 grocer 1 draper 2 parsons 2 clerks 2 lawyers and 3 or four nondescripts. All these but one have families to "take tea with" and there are a lot more single men to flirt with.

For the last 3 months we have been out every Sunday sketching. We seldom succeed in making the slightest resemblance to the thing we sit down to but it is wonderfully interesting. Next year we hope to send a lot home. Mrs Taylor has got another little girl.[9] Miss Knox, the third sister is going to follow after Mrs Couper's example and marry a rich old man of disgraceful character. She is just abt 17 and her intended (Capt. Rhodes)[10] has just put her to school. Waring has a good trade and fair health so has Mrs Taylor and the children—the health, not the trade. My cattle are nearly all in existence yet and instead of gaining I sha[ll] lose by them in consequence of keeping them so long. Meat sells for 5d a lb and I shall not get 3d. I should be ill off, but that Joe and John have given me the money which at

[8] In 1847, for instance, there were in Wellington 528 bachelors and 248 spinsters (Miller, p. 564).

[9] Margaret Russell Taylor, b. 22 February 1850, d. 28 April 1851. Another daughter, b. 21 September 1851, was then given the same name.

[10] William Barnard Rhodes (1807-78), a prominent citizen, whaler, trader, and landowner, who was associated with both Waring Taylor and William Couper in various enterprises. Though 'rich', he was neither 'old' nor 'of disgraceful character', he was among those who established the New Zealand Shipping Company, the New Zealand Insurance Company, and the Bank of New Zealand, and from 1853-73 was a member of the Provincial Council, Legislative Council, etc. He married first, Sarah King, daughter of a Wellington solicitor, in 1852, and secondly, Sarah Anne Moorhouse (Straubel ; *Encyclopaedia of New Zealand*).

first they lent me. With the increase I shall probably escape loss. With all this my novel stands still—it might have done so if I had /had/ nothing to do, for it is not want of time but want of freedom of mind that makes me unable to direct my attention to it. Meantime it grows in my head, for I never give up the idea. I have written abt a volume I suppose. Read this letter to Ellen Nussey and ask her what was the impending event, of importance to her, which she promised to tell me when she was "more sure abt it".[11]

There has been a man talking of cholera in England till he has made me melancholy—His "brother's wife's father" died of it at Bradford

Wellington 5 April 1850   Mary Taylor.[12]

LETTER 20

Mary Taylor to Charlotte Brontë, April 1850,[1] WS no. 550; text from MS. in Brontë Parsonage Museum, Haworth.

Dear Charlotte

I have set up shop! I am delighted with it it[2] as a whole —that is it is as pleasant or as little disagreeable as you can expect an employment to be that you earn your living by.

[11] Probably a reference to Ann Nussey's marriage on 26 September 1849, at the age of 54. Mary at first wrote 'she refuse', then crossed out 'refuse' in favour of 'promised'.

[12] Mary's remarks about shops, prices, etc., may be compared with Mrs Godley's for the same period. She remarks (28 April 1850) that 'there are really shops for everything' (Godley, *Letters,* p. 33), and says that 'meat to be sure is cheap enough, 5d a pound for the best joints'. On 15 September she comments 'We are quite delighted with the shopkeepers here, and indeed all the people of that class. We have made acquaintance with some very nice ones, and they are generally very civil' (pp. 102-3). If Mrs Godley went to make purchases at 'Miss Taylor's store' in Cuba Street, let us hope that it was Ellen Taylor, not Mary, who served her, for Mary might well have flashed out at the tone of such patronage.

[1] The Wellington postmark is 29 April 1850 ; of the Bradford stamp only '1850' can be read.

[2] Thus in MS.

The best of it is that your labour has some return and you are not forced to work on hopelessly without result. Du reste—it is very odd—I keep looking at myself with one eye while I'm using the other and I sometimes find myself in very queer positions. Yesterday I went along the shore past two wharves and several warehouses on a st. where I had never been before during all the 5 years I have been in Wellington. I opened the door of a long place filled with packages with passage up the middle and a row of high windows on one side.[3] At the far end of the room a man was writing at a desk beneath a window. I walked all the length of the room very slowly, for what I had come for had completely gone out of my head. Fortunately the man never heard me until I had recollected it. Then he got up and I asked him for some stone blue, saltpetre, tea, pickles, salt etc. He was very civil; I bought some things and asked for a note of them. He went to his desk again and I looked at some newspapers lying near. On the top was a circular fm Smith and Elder, containing notices of the most important new works. The first and longest was given to *Shirley* a book I had seen mentioned in the Manchester Examiner as written by Currer Bell.[4] I blushed all over; the man got up, folding the note. I pulled it out of his hand and set off to the door—looking odder than ever for a partner[5] had come in and was watching. The clerk said something about sending them and I said something too, I hope it was n't very silly—and took my departure.

I have seen some extracts from Shirley in which you talk of women working.[6] And this first duty, this great

[3] This was Bethune and Hunter's warehouse, at the corner of Corn-hill Street and Old Customhouse Street, then on the waterfront. Jonas Woodward, their accountant at this time, was the clerk whom Mary encountered.
[4] The *Manchester Examiner* reviewed *Shirley* on 7 November 1849.
[5] Kenneth Bethune or George Hunter junior.
[6] Mary felt strongly on this matter, lecturing both Charlotte and Ellen (Nussey) about it, and preaching the doctrine of work for women in her articles *The First Duty of Women* and in her novel *Miss Miles*. Charlotte also discussed it, especially in *Shirley* chapter 22 and *The Professor* chapter 25. See WS no. 452.

necessity you seem to think that *some* women may indulge in—if they give up marriage and don't make themselves too disagreeable to the other sex. You are a coward and a traitor. A woman who works is by that alone better than one who does not and a woman who does not happen to be rich and who *still* earns no money and does not wish to do so, is guilty of a great fault—almost a crime—A dereliction of duty which leads rapidly and almost certainly to all manner of degradation. It is very wrong of you to *plead* for toleration for workers on the ground of their being in peculiar circumstances and few in number or singular in disposition. Work or degradation is the lot of all except the very small number born to wealth.

For the last month I have really had a good excuse for not writing any more book. I have worked hard at something else. We have been moving, cleaning, shop-keeping until I was really tired every night—a wonder for me. It does me good, and I had much rather be tired than ennuyée. Have you seen Joe? or heard anything of John? There is a change gradually come over them in the last five years that I am only half acquainted with. Joe's gloom and John's wandering both shew wretched health, and Joe's cure seems to me very fantastic. By the eagerness with which he seeks to be married he evidently hopes more from the change than it will bring. It is certainly better to be married but to look forward to such great things is just insuring disappointment. Their business gives no subject for such depression and perhaps if they were poorer they would have more to care for. —We all here thrive wonderfully. Waring and his babies, Ellen and myself. Ellen is worst—that is least well. She was seriously ill on the passage out. Henry is in Sydney. I think he will learn Waring's trade and settle in Auckland.[7] John and Joe have promised to help him. Ellen is with me

[7] William Henry Taylor's life in New Zealand has not been traced, but he died at the Jubilee Home, Aramoho, Wanganui, on 7 December 1899. His occupation on the death certificate is given as 'carter', and his parents as 'unknown'. This suggests that the informant, the Coroner, knew nothing of Henry's relations in New Zealand, with whom presumably contact had long been lost.

or I with her; I cannot tell how our shop will turn out but I am as sanguine as ever. Meantime we certainly amuse ourselves better than if we had nothing to do. We *like* it, that's the truth.—By the Cornelia[8] we are going to send our sketches and fern leaves. You must look at them and it will need all your eyes to understand them for they are a mass of confusion. They are all within 2 miles of Wellington and some of them rather like; Ellen's sketch of me especially. During the last 6 months I have seen more "society" than in all the last 4 years. Ellen is half the reason of my being invited and my improved circumstances besides. There is no one worth mentioning particularly. The women are all ignorant and narrow and the men selfish. They are of a decent honest kind and *some* intel[lige]nt and able. Mrs Taylor's parson (Woodward) [is] the only *literary* man we know and he seems to have fair sense   This was the clerk I bought the stone blue of. We have just got a mechanic's Institute and weekly lectures delivered there.[9] It is amusing to see people trying to find out whether or not it is fashionable and proper to patronise it. Some how it seems it is. I think I have told you all this before, which shows I have got to the end of my news. Your next letter to me ought to bring me good news; more cheerful than the last. You will some how get drawn out of your hole and find interests among your fellow creatures. Do you know that living among people with whom you have not the slightest interest in common is just like living alone, or worse. Ellen Nussey is the only one you can talk to, that I know of at least. Give my love to her, and to Miss Wooler if you have the opportunity. I am writing this on just such a night as you will likely read it. Rain and storm—coming winter and a glowing fire[10]—Ours

---

[8] This 'splendid new barque' of 372 tons, advertised all through April, finally sailed on 18 May.

[9] Lecture subjects included Phrenology, Astronomy, Terrestrial Magnetism, Zoology, and the Immortality of the Soul. Woodward spoke on Banking and Currency.

[10] Charlotte Godley comments on the Wellington gales of April 23-30, adding, like Mary, 'what can people want beyond a fire to sit by?' (Godley, *Letters,* pp. 31-4).

is on the ground wood, no fender or irons—no matter we
are very comfortable

Pag.

The presence of Ellen Taylor had obviously altered
Mary's life dramatically for the better. Two more long letters
went off to Yorkshire in August 1850.

LETTER 21

*Mary and Ellen Taylor to Charlotte Brontë, 13 August
1850, WS nos. 583 and 584; text from MS. in Berg Collection, New York Public Library.*[1]

Dear Charlotte

After waiting about six months we have just got Shirley.[2]
It was landed from the Constantinople one Monday afternoon just in the thick of our preparations for a "small
party" for the next day. We stopped spreading /red/ blankets over everything (N. Zealand way of arranging the
room) and opened the box and red[3] all the letters. Soyers
Housewife[4] and Shirley were there all right but Miss Martineau's book[5] was not. In its place was a silly child's tale
called Edward Orland.[6] This is Joe's fault no doubt for I

---

[1] This is a single letter, begun by Mary and finished by Ellen,
although WS print it as letters 584 and 583.

[2] *Shirley* was published on 26 October 1849. The *Constantinople*
arrived in Wellington on 27 July 1850. Mrs Godley noted on 29
August 1850 that the merchant W. M. Bannatyne 'has lately had
out a case of new books of which he has given us the run', *Shirley*
being among them (Godley, *Letters*, p. 93).

[3] Thus in MS.

[4] Alexis Soyer, *The Modern Housewife or Menagère*. London, 1849.

[5] Probably Harriet Martineau's *Eastern Life*, 1848, which Charlotte
was reading with 'great pleasure' on 1 October 1849 (WS no. 479).

[6] *Edward Orland, or, Truth and Untruth*, by M-, Heckmondwike.
London, 1847. This is a sentimental religious tale about a boy
who was kind to worms and flowers, and therefore came to a
good end. Joe Taylor perhaps knew something of the anonymous
'Margarette' who wrote it, since Heckmondwike is near Gomersal.

see in one of yr letters you suspect him of it.—On Tuesday
we stayed up dancing till 3 or 4 o'cl. what for I can't imagine. However it was a piece of business done. On Wednesday
I began Shirley and continued in a curious confusion of
mind till now principally abt the handsome foreigner who
was nursed in our house when I was a little girl.[7]—By the
way you've put him in the servant's bedroom. You make
us all talk much as I think we shd have done if we'd ventured to speak at all—What a little lump of perfection you've
made me![8] There is a strange feeling in reading it of hearing
us all talking.[9] I have not seen the matted hall and painted
parlour windows so plain these 5 years.[10] But my Father is
not like. He hates well enough and perhaps loves too but he
is not honest enough. It was from my father I learnt not to
marry for money nor to tolerate any one who did and he
never wd advise any one to do so or fail to speak with
contempt of those who did. Shirley is much more interesting
than J. Eyre—who indeed never interests you at all until
she has something to suffer. All through this last novel there
is so much more life and stir—that it leaves you far more

[7] In *Shirley,* Robert Gérard Moore, wounded by the Luddite Mill
hands, is nursed by the Yorke family at Briarmains (i.e., by the
Taylors at the Red House)—and is given 'the best bed in the
house' (chapter 32). The situation of the room is indicated in
chapter 33. It is upstairs ; above the entrance hall 'there was a
gallery, and there was a passage ; at the end of that passage
Martin [i.e., Joseph Taylor] paused before a door and tapped' to
take Caroline Helstone in to see the patient.

[8] For a discussion of the Taylor-Yorke family in *Shirley,* see the
General Introduction.

[9] Spelt 'talkking' by mistaken line division.

[10] Described in chapter 3. The windows are now in the Brontë
Parsonage Museum. Mrs Gaskell reported that Charlotte told
her 'that, before publication, she had sent those parts of the novel
in which these remarkable persons are introduced, to one of the
sons ; and his reply, after reading it, was simply that "she had
not drawn them strong enough" ' (Gaskell, *Life,* p. 414). According to Edward Taylor, Mary's nephew, when his father
Joshua (III) read the novel, he said 'Either my brother Joe wrote
that book or someone who knew him intimately' (*BST* Vol. 15
No. 4, 1969, p. 311).

to remember than the other. Did you go to London abt this too.[11] What for? I see by a letter of yours to M. Dixon[12] that you have been. You shd scold Joe for not sending Household Education.[13] I wanted to contradict some of yr opinions, now I can't. As to when I'm coming home you may well ask. I have wished for 15 years to begin to earn my own living last April I began to try. It is too soon yet to say with what success. I am wofully ignorant terribly wanting in tact and obstinately lazy, and almost too old to mend. Luckily there is no other chance for me; so I must work. Ellen takes to it kindly it gratifies a deep ardent wish of hers as of mine and she is habitually industrious. For *her*—10 yrs younger, our shop will be a blessing. She may possibly secure an independence—and skill to keep it and use it, before the prime of life is past. As to my writings you may ask well ask[14] the Fates abt that too. I can give you no information. I write a page now and then and never forget or get strange to what I have written. When I read it over it looks very interesting.

My Dear Miss Brontë

I shall tell you everything I can think of, since you said [in] one of your letters to Pag that you wished me to write to you—I have been here a year it seems a much shorter time—and yet I have thought more and done more than I ever did in my life before—When we arrived Henry and I were in such a hurry to leave the ship[15] that we didn't wait to be fetched, but got into the first boat that came alongside, when we landed we enquired where Waring lived but hadn't walked far before we met him; I had never seen him before, but he guessed we were the cousins he expected and so caught us and took us along with him; Mary soon joined

---

[11] Charlotte stayed in London from 29 November to 15 December 1849 at the home of her publisher, George Smith, and met various notables (Gérin, pp. 401-13).

[12] Mary Dixon ; further evidence of the degree to which letters were circulated round the group.

[13] Not traced.

[14] Thus in MS.

[15] The *Jane Catherine* arrived in Wellington on 16 August 1849.

us and we went home together; at first I thought Mary was
not the least altered but [after] I had seen her for about a
week I thought she looked rather older—The first night
Mary and I sat up till 2 a.m. talking—Next day we went to
tea—to the Knoxes Waring's new relations you have no
doubt heard of them, the Dr. is an idle fool and his wife not
very much better, he might earn his living if he would—but
he wont[16]—In a few days we began to talk about doing
something it seemed the only thing for Henry to do was to
buy sheep and go and keep them in the country, he went to
look at Rangitiki a large district bought of the natives,[17] it
is somewhere on the West Coast between here and Taranaki;
he came back and said it was too wet for sheep but he
thought he would have to go there—In November he went
to Sydney to buy the sheep; but he found freights to[o]
high then so he settled to wait a bit; and he is waiting yet,
that is he hasn't come back. and we haven't heard a word
of or from him for 5 months, he must have gone into the
bush, but if he has he ought to have told us I wish he'd
come back—Mary and I settled we would do something together and we talked for a fortnight before we decided
whether we would have a school or shop, it ended in favour
of the shop—Waring thought we had better be quiet, and I
believe he still thinks we are doing it for amusement, but he
never refuses to help us, he *is* teaching us book keeping, and
he buys things for us now and then. Mary gets as fierce as a
dragon[18] and goes to all the wholesale stores and looks at
things, gets, patterns samples etc. and asks prices, and then
comes home and we talk it over and then she goes again and
buys what we want, she says the people are always civil to
her—Our keeping shop astonishes every body here, I believe

[16] For details about Dr Knox which give a contrary impression, see
Stevens, in *New Zealand Libraries*, October 1968.

[17] The Rangitikei block of some 200,000 acres between the Rangitikei and Turakina rivers was bought by Donald McLean, Land
Purchase Commissioner, in May 1849.

[18] Apparently a characteristic trait of Mary's ; cf. Martha Taylor's
phrases 'our dragon' and 'fierce as a tiger' in Letter no. 2, April
1842.

they think we do it for fun, some think we shall make nothing of it, or that we shall get tired; and all laugh at us. Before
I left home I used to be afraid of being laughed at, but now
it has very little effect upon me—

Mary and I are settled together now, I cant do without
Mary and she couldn't get on by herself—I built the house
we live in, and we made the plan ourselves so it suits us;
we take it in turns to serve in the shop and keep to[19]
accounts, and do the house work, I mean Mary takes the
shop for a week and I the kitchen and then we change—I
think we shall do very well if no more severe earthquakes
come and if we can prevent fire, when a wooden house takes
fire it doesn't stop and we have got an oil cask about as high
as I am, that would help it, if some sparks go out at the
chimney top the shingles are in danger—The last earthquake
but one about a fortnight ago threw down 2 medicine bottles
that were standing on the table and made other things jingle,
but did no damage, if we have nothing worse than that I
dont care, but I dont want the chimney to come down it
would [cost] £10 to build it up again—Mary is making me
stop because it is nearly 9 p.m. and we are going to Warings
to supper—Good-bye yours truly

                Ellen Taylor—
           Wellington   August 13, 1850

LETTER 22

Mary Taylor to Ellen Nussey, 15 August 1850, WS no.
585; text from MS. in Berg Collection, New York Public
Library. Postmark illegible.

Dear Ellen

Last Monday we stopped working to open a box and
read letters.[1] Your pretty thing whatever is the name of it?

---

[19] Thus in MS.

[1] Mary is describing to Ellen the same excitement at the arrival of
the *Constantinople's* mail which she had already outlined to
Charlotte in Letter 21.

came almost the first and fine amusement it was to open it. What veritable old maids you and Charlotte must be grown if you really use such a thing. Ellen and I pulled out all the things, one after another and disputed for them. The stay-lace was particularly amusing! I have not seen such a thing this 5 years. But the best was the garters. I have had almost a daily lecture from Ellen because my stockings wrinkled owing to my having been reduced to two bits of tape for the last six months, and being too stingy to buy any more and too idle to knit them. Ellen says you might have known.

Your letter is the most cheerful I have had from you. I suppose "Charlotte" was or had been with you; or was going to be.[2] It contained more news too than any I have received by this ship. Ann's marriage[3] does not seem to have made you more uncomfortable—perhaps the reverse. Was this the news you hinted at in your last but which you d[id] not tell me? I had guessed it was yr own marriage that was going to be! I had imagined too that Miss Gorham must be the daughter of the Revd. Mr G. who is having such a quarrel with the bishop of Exeter.[4] Which of course I highly approve of tho' I don't know what it's all about. I wish you or Charlotte wd give me some particulars of her last London visit. The account of the first one was most interesting.[5] Ellen is roasting her toes and discussing how little she'll be content with. It seems to be abt £200 a year tho' it is doubt-ful if this will do. It is blowing cold and rain and hail—just to make a fire comfortable. She (Ellen) chatters like a pie and the theme is how much we must have before we go home again. We think it possible to buy and send goods out

2 Charlotte visited Ellen in October 1849 (WS nos. 481, 483, 484), and Ellen visited Charlotte in January 1850 (WS nos. 513, 520).

3 Ann Nussey had married Robert Clapham, of Batley, in Septem-ber 1849.

4 Ellen Nussey's friend Mary Gorham was no relation of George Cornelius Gorham (1787-1857), at this time Vicar of Brampton Speke, Devon. In 1847 he was refused institution to the office by the Bishop of Exeter on account of his liberal views on baptism, but won his appeal to the Privy Council in 1850. He published *The Great Gorham Case* in 1850. See pp. 111-12.

5 Charlotte's letter of 4 September 1848, see Appendix E.

here after 4 or 5 years experience—in shop keeping. You
and Charlotte ought to be on the other side the table to hear
all the nonsense. For the last month or two Ellen has been
very well and I too. Before that time she was often very
poorly and I had repeatedly tic douloureux in the face. We
were frightened shy and anxious. Neither the shyness nor the
anxiety are at an end as we very well know but *we know*
what we have to contend with and can never feel so thick a
mist round us as there was when we first began. I wish I cd
give you some account of the amount of our success but the
time is as yet too short to pronounce. The gist of the matter
is that John and Joe have lent me £100 and given me £300.
Ellen's means are rather less.

Besides nonsense we talk over other things that I never cd
talk about before she came. Some of them had got to look so
strange I used to think sometimes I had dreamt them.
Charlotte's books were of this kind. Politics were another
thing where I had all the interest to myself and a number of
opinions of my own I had got so used to keep to myself that
at last I thought one side of my head filled with crazy stuff.

Is it that your brothers won't give you money that pre-
vents you coming out?—You shd *plague* them till they are
glad to be rid of you. But I fancy you write more hopefully
than you did before. And yet you seem almost turned out of
doors by the new arrangement. In fact there is only your
mother that really belongs to you in it.

Joe's admiration of Miss Ringrose is amusing—if it is so.
Is she German? or half German? Have you seen or heard of
Halle's chamber concerts? His father was my music master
and a genius. His mother is living with him. I have some
notion that you are near them tho' I believe in point of fact
you are as far off as I am. There was a girl of 14-20 whom
I shd much like to hear of.[6]

---

[6] Christian Friedrich Andreas Hallé, Mary's music teacher in
Hagen (see Letter 12) died in 1848. His son Karl Friedrich
(1819-95) settled in England that year, and from 1850 onwards
was associated with musical enterprises in Manchester. His
mother, however, remained in Hagen ; his only sister, Bertha
Anna, b. 1830, joined him in Manchester in 1866 (Hallé).

For some reason—or rather for no reason I think my hopes this afternoon are peculiarly vivid about coming home again. All the news by [the] last vessel has been good and reading the letters has brought it all vividly before me. Keep yourself well and happy, you and Charlotte till I come and above all don't turn sulky. We shall meet again yet.

You have both suffered Charlotte especially. I am older in that way too, but there is sweet in the orange yet—at least I think so.

Mary Taylor

Wellington.   Aug. 15   1850

It was probably the arrival of the letters sent from Wellington in April that Charlotte reported to Ellen Nussey on 14 October: 'I have had a letter from Mary Taylor lately—she is well happy and prosperous—her shop thriving—herself content—I am glad of this ' (WS no. 610).

The August bundle arrived in February 1851, whereupon Charlotte and Ellen, both recipients, exchanged news. 'I also received a letter from Mary Taylor written, not in high spirits—but still shewing hopeful prospects; also one from Ellen Taylor by which I think her health must be better' (WS no. 645).

Mary's next letter is to Ellen Nussey, in March 1851.

LETTER 23

Mary Taylor to Ellen Nussey, 11 March 1851, WS no. 647; text from MS. in Berg Collection, New York Public Library. No postmarks.

Wellington Mar 11 1851

Dear Ellen

Your letter made me ashamed of my self, as it reminded me how long I have neglected answering your letters. I am now going to answer it sentence by sentence as I shd do if I could sit down and write the moment I read it. I am glad Joe has taken it into his head to marry some one who knows

my friends and who is therefore likely to learn to think
well of me.[1] I hope you will both you and Charlotte Brontë,
keep up yr acquaintance with Amelia and each of you send
news of the other as good as you can find to write.

It must be gloomy indeed for Charlotte to see her Father's
health declining.[2] It is frightful to see death coming to take
the last, and one can scarcely calculate the effects on a
weakened painstruck mind like Charlotte's. It seems to me
as if the triumphs she has had, had only opened to her new
sources of pain. She thinks or rather feels more of the
criticism than the praise. In spite of her strenuous endeavour
she cannot look at the cheerful side for sadness at present
with her. You yourself seem in much better spirits—How do
you manage it? I wish you were sitting here by this quiet
candlelight and I wd talk to you by the hour of how we were
getting on. How we were looking for a ship from England
—what was sold today. How intend to do when the said
ship comes and we have no room or next to none to put the
things she is to bring. How eagerly we open the packages
and scold for all the things that are not according to order.
How we work! and lift and carry and knock boxes open as
if we were carpenters by trade; and sit down in the midst of
the mess when we're quite tired, and ask what time it is, and
find it is the middle of the afternoon and we've forgotten our
dinner! And then we settle to ham some tea and eggs, and
go on reading letters all the time we're eating, and don't give
over working till bedtime and take a new number of D.
Copperfield to bed with us and drop asleep at the second
page.[3]

In quieter times we are somewhat lazy. There is not more
than employment for one. As we don't keep the house particularly tidy the other one might do a great deal. But some
how not being forced to it we never do it. We ought to go
out and draw (—ask Joe to shew you our last wonders in
that way) but we find it dull going alone. Then perhaps we

---

[1] Joseph Taylor married Amelia Ringrose in September 1850.

[2] Mr Brontë (b. 1777) suffered a severe cold in July-August 1850,
but he lived until 1861.

[3] Appearing in monthly parts from May 1849 to November 1850.

ought to write but dont like for we might possibly be interrupted. We see some company—not much, but I think much better than we shd in the same circumstances in England. Classes are forced to mix more here, or there wd be no society at all. This circumstance is much to our advantage for there are not many educated people of our standing. The women are the same every where—never educated and so far as female friends go I think our present set have as much principle and kindness as most of those we left while they have certainly more energy. You need not tell the Birstalians my opinion of them. Probably they are not worse than other women but never called upon to stand alone or allowed to act for themselves, of course they lose their wits in time.— Don't lose my letter in church lane or thereabouts.[4] I. Nussey[5] writes to know if it is true that Miss Brontë was jilted by a curate—or by 3 in succession, I forget which— pray ask her![6] I have told people of my acquaintance with the writer of J. Eyre and gained myself a great literary reputation thereby. Mama has written to Waring abusing Miss Brontë for writing Shirley[7] and Waring thereupon asked to read it. He says the characters are all unfaithful and stoutly denies that ever my Father talked talked[8] broad Yorkshire. He seems to have forgotten home altogether. He once described minutely how he shd like to have a room finished and furnished if he were rich; and he described our old dining room in every point and s[ai]d he did n[o]t know he'd ever seen such a room! He has a house of his own now and wife and children none of whom ever saw Gomersal nor ever will do! We're getting old El[len] and out of date! Fare thee well till another quiet evening.

M. Taylor

[4] Church Lane, leading from Gomersal Hill Top down to Birstall Church.

[5] Isabel Nussey, Ellen's second cousin, whom Joseph Taylor flirted with in 1845.

[6] Doubtless this rumour derived from Charlotte's rough handling of the curates in *Shirley*.

[7] Mrs Taylor cannot have enjoyed her portrait as 'Mrs Yorke'.

[8] Thus in MS.

In June 1851 Charlotte several times referred to letters from Mary; one was 'cheerfully written—but she does not give a very good account of Ellen's health' (WS no. 675).

On 21 October Charlotte summarized the New Zealand news for the benefit of Miss Wooler (WS no. 713): 'Letters have been recently received from Mary and Ellen Taylor in New Zealand—I wished I could have shewn one of these to you—it gives such a thoroughly characteristic notion of their way of life. According to the description it contained of their sitting-room—neither of them were in the way of meriting the Roe-Head Neatness Prize: they deserve on the contrary loss of tickets and an early adjournment to bed. More shame to them'.

By January 1852, her Yorkshire friends had realized that Ellen Taylor must be seriously ill; on the 5th Charlotte wrote to Ellen Nussey: 'Poor Ellen Taylor! I fear hers will not be a long life—Should she die in New Zealand—it will be most sad for Mary—' (WS no. 736).

Ellen died of consumption on 27 December 1851. Mary wrote by the first available mail, that carried by the *Clara*, of the New Zealand Line of Packets, which left Wellington on 9 January 1852. Charlotte wrote to Ellen with the news in a letter which she dated 'March 4th'. But up to 24 April, the *New Zealand Journal*, a fortnightly published in London, was noting the date of the latest mail from Wellington as 7 December 1851; in the issue of 8 May, this was changed to 8 January 1852. The *Clara's* mail, therefore, arrived between 24 April and 8 May 1852. Perhaps Charlotte meant to put May 4th (WS no. 754; text from MS. in Huntington Library).

The news of E. Taylor's death came to me last week in a letter from Mary—a long letter—which wrung my heart so—in its simple, strong, truthful emotion—I have only ventured to read it once. It ripped up half-scarred wounds with terrible force—the death-bed was just the same—breath failing etc.

She fears she shall now in her dreary solitude become "a stern, harsh, selfish woman"—this fear struck home—again and again I have felt it for myself—and what is *my* position—to Mary's? I should break out in energetic wishes that she would return to England—if reason would permit me to believe that prosperity and happiness would there await her—but I see no such prospect. May God help her as only God can help!

Soon the Hunsworth family were also passing on the news of Ellen Taylor's last hours. Charlotte sent letters on to Ellen Nussey on 18 May: 'I enclose Mary's letter announcing Ellen's death and Ellen's two last letters—sorrowful documents—all of them. I received them this morning from Hunsworth without any note or directions where to send them, but I think—if I mistake not—Amelia in a previous note told me to transmit them to you' (WS no. 768).

The next of Mary's letters to survive is written to Charlotte four months after Ellen Taylor's death, in April 1852.

LETTER 24

Mary Taylor to Charlotte Brontë, 1852,[1] *WS no. 763; text from MS. in Berg Collection, New York Public Library.*

Dear Charlotte

I began a letter to you one bitter cold evening last week, but it turned out such a sad one that I have left it and begun again. I am sitting all alone in my own house, or rather what is to be mine when I've paid for it. I bought it of Henry, when Ellen died, shop and all, and carry on by my self. I have made up my mind not to get any assistance; I have not too much work and the annoyance of having an unsuitable companion was too great to put up with without necessity. I find now that it was Ellen that made me so busy

[1] The Wellington postmark is illegible except for '1852', but the Keighley postmark is 27 October 1852. CB sent the letter on to EN on 31 October (WS no. 793).

and without her to nurse I have plenty of time. I have begun
to keep the house very tidy; it makes it less desolate. I take
great interest in my trade—as much as I could do in anything
that was not *all* pleasure. But the best part of my life is the
excitement of arrivals from England. Reading all the news,
written and printed, is like living another life quite separate
from this one. The old letters are strange, very, when I *begin*
to read them but quite familiar notwithstanding. So are all
the books and newspapers, tho I never see a human being to
whom it wd ever occur to me to mention anything I read in
them. I see your nom de guerre in them sometimes. I saw a
criticism on the preface to the second edition of Wuthering
heights.[2] I saw it among the notables who attended Thackeray's lectures.[3] I have seen it somehow connected with Sir
J. K. Shuttleworth.[4] Did he want to marry you or only to
lionize you? *or was it somebody else?*

Your life in London is a "new country" to me which I
cannot even picture to myself. You seem to like it—at least
some things in it, and yet your late letters to Mrs J. Taylor
talk of low spirits and illness.[5] "What's the matter with you
now" as my mother used to say, as if it were the twentieth
time in a fortnight. It is really melancholy that now, in the
prime of life in the flush of your hard earned prosperity you
can't be well! Did not Miss Martineau improve you? If she
did not why not try her and her plan again?[6] But I suppose

[2] Thus in MS. The second edition of *Wuthering Heights and Agnes
Grey,* by Ellis and Acton Bell, with a 'biographical notice of the
authors, a selection from their best literary remains, and a preface
by Currer Bell', was published on 10 December 1850.

[3] Charlotte visited London from 28 May to 27 June 1851, and
attended four of Thackeray's six lectures on the English Humour-
ists (Gérin, p. 474).

[4] Sir James Kay-Shuttleworth, of Gawthorpe Hall, near Burnley.
Charlotte visited him at Windermere in August 1850, and there
met Mrs Gaskell (Gérin, pp. 419-26, 441-9).

[5] Another indication that letters went round the group ; this time it
is Joseph Taylor's wife Amelia who has sent on news.

[6] Harriet Martineau, whom Charlotte visited at Ambleside in
December 1850 (Gérin, pp. 456-62). The 'plan' is perhaps the
experiment in mesmerism which Charlotte underwent while there
(WS no. 637).

if you had hope and energy to try, you wd be well.—Well it's nearly dark and you will surely be well when you read this so what's the use of writing? I shd like well to have some details of your life but how can I hope for it? I have often tried to give you a picture of mine but I have not the skill. I get a heap of details, most paltry in themselves and not enough to give you an idea of the whole. O for one hour's talk! You are getting too far off and beginning to look strange to me. Do you look as you used to do I wonder? What do you and Ellen Nussey talk about when you meet? There! it's dark.

Sunday night. I have let the vessel go that was to take this. As there [are] others going soon I did not much care. I am in the height of cogitation whether to send for some worsted stockings etc. They will come next year at this time and who can tell what I shall want then, or shall be doing! Yet hitherto we have sent such orders and have guessed or known pretty well what we shd want. I have just been looking over a list 4 pages long in Ellen's handwriting. These things ought to come by the next vessel or part of them at least. Then tired of that I began to read some pages of "my book" intending to write some more but went on reading for pleasure. I often do this and find it very interesting indeed. It does not get on fast tho. I have written about 1 vol. and a half. Its full of music, poverty, disputing, politics, and original views of life. I can't for the life of me bring the lover into it nor tell what he's to do when he comes. Of the men generally I can never tell what they'll do next. The women I understand pretty well, and rare tracasserie there is among them,—they are perfectly *feminine* in that respect at least.[7]

I am just now in a state of famine. No books and no news from England for this 2 months. I am thinking of visiting a circula[ting] library from sheer dullness. If I had more time I should get m[elan]choly No one can prize activity more than I do little interest [though] there is in it. I never long am without it but a gloom comes over me. The

---

[7] This criticism of *Miss Miles* is very fair.

cloud seems to be always there behind me and never quite out of sight but when I keep on at a good rate. Fortunately the more I work the better I like it—I shall take to scrubbing the floor before its dirty and polishing pans on the outside in my old age.—It is the only thing that gives me an appetite for dinner.

I suppose if the vessel coming from England is not lost I shall soon be too busy to write if the last vessel were sailing that ever was to go. So take this in anticipation as I can't write an answer to your letters until they get too old to answer.   Pag.

Give my love to Ellen Nussey.

Later in the year further letters arrived; on 12 August Charlotte reported on one (WS no. 781, misdated as 13th; MS. at Brotherton Library, Leeds). 'A letter has just been received from Mary Taylor which no doubt will be duly sent you—She seems to write in somewhat better spirits— she had got the box containing the bonnets etc which you selected—and expresses herself most thoroughly satisfied with Ellen Nussey's choice—She says Amelia could not have put the affair in better hands.'

On 5 October Charlotte referred to two more letters of Mary's which Ellen had passed on to her; and when Letter 24 arrived she sent it on to Ellen almost at once (31 October). 'I have just got a letter from New Zealand which I enclose—it made me sad—I cannot help earnestly wishing that Mary were back in England—if one could see but the slightest chance of an opening for her making her way' (WS no. 793).

A year passed before the date of Mary's next surviving letter. It deals with an episode in Ellen Nussey's life of which the first mention occurs in this same October letter of Charlotte's, and which was of considerable importance to the three friends. The Reverend Francis Upjohn, Vicar of Gorleston near Great Yarmouth, and his wife made to Ellen a proposal which Charlotte summarized as follows: 'That you should go and spend some time with them on a sort of experiment visit—that if the result were mutually satisfactory—they would wish in a sense to adopt you—with the prospect of leaving you property—amount of course indefinite' (WS no. 793). Charlotte also felt that Mrs Upjohn seemed to be a 'warm-hearted, good-natured woman', who was making this gesture to Ellen out of 'affectionate remembrance'. But she warned Ellen that 'to leave your own home and Mother for the society of two elderly invalids is a step demanding caution'.

The Rev. Francis Upjohn was the second son of Francis Upjohn, of a noted jewellery and watchmaking firm in London, and was born in 1787. Before taking Holy Orders he had been a captain in a Dragoon regiment. He entered Queens' College Cambridge in 1826, took his M.A. in 1833, and became Vicar of Gorleston in 1841, his parish being just within the Suffolk boundary to the south of Great Yarmouth. His first wife, Catherine Mary (née Tookie) died in 1840 at the age of eighty-four. In May 1842 he married again, his wife being Sarah, the fifty year old spinster sister of that George Cornelius Gorham whose 'quarrel with the bishop of Exeter' Mary Taylor 'highly' approved of, as she wrote on 15 August 1850 (Letter 22). There were no children in either marriage. Another Gorham sister, Christiana Elizabeth, had married in 1819 the Rev. Dr Joseph Holmes, at that date a Fellow and Tutor of Queens', and later Headmaster of Leeds Grammar School from 1830 to 1854.

The Rev. Upjohn was not only Vicar of St Andrew's, Gorleston, but Rector of Southtown and Westtown, parishes annexed to it but by 1845 'decayed', according to White's *Norfolk*. C. J. Palmer records that the value in the Rating Book was £381 at the beginning of Upjohn's incumbency, with the great tithes of Southtown, and tithes of wood, hay and clover in Gorleston. By 1854, when the gross income was £400, Upjohn had sold the Rectorial tithes; at the 1851 census his curate occupied the Gorleston Vicarage, from which it seems that Upjohn had already become the 'non-resident incumbent' which he is described as being in later records right up to his death in London in 1874, at the age of eighty-seven.

It is tempting to assume with Mary Taylor that Ellen
Nussey's friend Mary Gorham was related to the Rev.
George Cornelius Gorham, since this would account for the
acquaintance between Mrs Upjohn and Ellen, and for the
'affectionate remembrance' of Charlotte's comment. Certainly the Rev. George Cornelius had a sister Mary (1783-
1851), but Ellen's friend was the daughter of John Gorham,
and in June 1852 had married the Rev. Thomas Swinton
Hewitt, in the family's parish church at West Wittering,
Sussex. Ellen signed the register, as did Mary's brother the
Rev. John Gorham, Canon of nearby Aldingbourne. As for
the Cornelius Gorhams, a search of their records, well docu-
mented back to 1700, has not revealed any link whatever
between the two families.

Another tempting assumption is that the connection between Ellen and the Upjohns derives from the Joseph
Holmes family at Leeds, since Mrs Holmes and Mrs Upjohn were sisters. A great-aunt of Ellen's had married a
William Holmes of Hampsthwaite, and their son, the Reverend Nussey Holmes, held the Curacy of Weston, near
Leeds, from 1789, and was appointed Incumbent of Farnley
Chapel in the parish of Leeds in 1804. The Reverend Dr
Joseph Holmes came, however, from Market Weighton, and
search has failed to establish any connection. The origin
of Mrs Upjohn's 'affectionate remembrance' of Ellen must
therefore remain obscure.

The Upjohn proposal is first mentioned in Charlotte's
letter of 31 October 1852, already quoted, at which point
her reaction was not unfavourable, though she thought the
idea 'peculiar', and fraught with difficulties. She referred at
that time also to Mrs Upjohn's having 'a sort of vivacity of
temperament and feeling . . . which seems to have had
genuineness to survive such a catalogue of afflictions as
rarely fall in succession on one human being. Poor woman!
She has been sorely tried.' The matter is further discussed in
an undated letter about the same time (WS no. 794) which
indicates the degree of the Brontës' concern that 'something
advantageous' to Ellen might spring from the suggestion:

Thanks for your letter, you are right to go, and to go soon. I somehow wish you to get it over; I hope you won't be *very* long away this time, whatever you eventually decide on. I am not sanguine. If your affections bind or incline you to Mr and Mrs Upjohn you *ought* to stay; if they do not, I know from your nature you never will be able to get on. I feel certain that for the mere prospect of "future advantage" you could no more live with them than I could, you will see how it is. I quite anticipate difficulties, but *you will see.* I wish the "future advantage" were more defined; would it be a legacy of £40 or £50 per ann. or what? When I mentioned it to papa, he remarked that it was not *delicately* expressed. I could not but agree in this remark. He seems, however, most specially solicitous that you should try the adventure, and thinks unimportant objections ought not lightly to weigh with you.

In November Charlotte paid a visit to Ellen at Brookroyd, when the affair must have been discussed. It was probably about this time that Ellen sent off to Mary the letter to which Mary reacted so positively in May 1843 (Letter 25). Ellen decided, however, 'not to go to Yarmouth until after Christmas' (WS no. 804), owing to her mother's illness. Mr Brontë was 'glad on the whole to hear you are not going to Yarmouth just yet; he thinks you should be cautious' (WS no. 805).
On 15 December Charlotte referred to the matter again, in more doubtful terms: 'I return Mrs Upjohn's note which is highly characteristic, and not, I fear, of good omen for the comfort of your visit. There must be something wrong in herself as well as in her servants' (WS no. 807). Twice in January 1853 Charlotte inquired about Ellen's 'plans in regard to Mrs Upjohn' (WS nos. 811, 814), and these must have been discussed also during Ellen's visit to Haworth in February. Soon after this, Charlotte wrote 'Mrs Upjohn is really too trying. I do hope by this time you have heard from her . . . . This suspense, and this constant change of

plan is very wearisome and wearing' (WS no. 826). Mrs
Upjohn was still 'inconclusive' on 4 March (WS no.
831); on 10 March Charlotte noted that 'Mrs Upjohn is really a
strange person—but I begin to think that when you actually go to Gorleston, you will find her better than expecta-
tion—she cannot be much worse' (WS no. 833).

On 22 March, there is further exasperation: 'Mrs Upjohn
really carries her protractions and vacillations a little too
far . . . . It is a trial of Job to be thus moved backward and
forward by this most luckless of Mistresses and her tribe of
reprobate servants' (WS no. 834). By 6 April, Charlotte
was even more decided:

> I return Mrs Upjohn's letter. She has indeed acted very
> strangely, but it is evident to me that there is something
> very wrong either in herself, her husband, or her domes-
> tic arrangements, or (what is perhaps most probable)
> in all three . . . . The grounds for expecting permanent
> good some time ago assumed a very unsubstantial ap-
> pearance; the hope of present pleasure, I fear, would
> have turned out equally fallacious. Indeed I now feel
> little confidence in either comfort or credit ensuing from
> the connection in any shape (WS no. 838).

On 13 April Charlotte told Miss Wooler: 'Ellen Nussey's
visit to Yarmouth seems for the present given up—and
really—all things considered—I think the circumstance is
scarcely to be regretted—it seemed a doubtful kind of
prospect' (WS no. 840). Charlotte stayed with Ellen at
Birstall on the way back from her visit to Mrs Gaskell.
Soon after reaching Haworth early in May, she received
'without the slightest sentiment of wonder' the news of a
'fresh put-off' (WS no. 846). By 19 May, however there
was a definite arrangement that Ellen should go to the
Upjohns for a trial month. She was to be guided in her
decision by what she found there. A cryptic reference to
their house being 'haunted', as Ellen's brother-in-law Mr
Clapham supposed, is unexplained (WS no. 847). On 27
May, Charlotte heard that Ellen had 'safely arrived at last',

but at a house where, by a typical 'sort of miscalculation', the hostess was away from home! Other disconcerting oddities were mentioned: 'I do not much like to hear', wrote Charlotte, 'of that supposed infection of the brain', and she omitted the *Leader* from the usual bundle of papers which she sent on to Ellen, thinking that it would not 'suit Mr Upjohn' (WS no. 849). At this date Upjohn was sixty-six, and might perhaps have proved to be a 'pleasant, well-informed companion' for the thirty-six year old Ellen, as Charlotte tried to hope. But by early June the failure of the trial was clear. Ellen had 'a hard time of it and some rough experience' with the 'strange, unhappy people at Gorleston', and fled to her brother Joshua's Vicarage at Oundle before her month was up (WS nos. 852, 853, 854, 855). Her description of the visit, sent off to Mary Taylor on 12 August, was 'amusing', at least, but Mary was 'right glad' that Ellen came back safely (Letter 26).

The rest of the story is unknown, except that by 1864 the Rev. Mr Upjohn was no longer resident at Gorleston. His will, drawn up in London in 1866, appointed as an executor his wife's nephew, the Rev. Francis Graeme Holmes, one of the five clerical sons of the Rev. Joseph Holmes. (Holmes's only daughter had married George Cornelius Gorham's son in 1855). At his death in 1874, Upjohn's effects were valued at 'under £8000'; had Ellen Nussey, then, acceded to his proposal, she would have worked for twenty-one years for the 'future advantage' of her legacy. Indeed, the period would have been longer, since Mrs Upjohn lived on to be eighty-nine, not dying until 1881.

In view of the history of this Upjohn affair, Mary Taylor's forthright and independent judgment of it at its very inception in October 1852 is to be heartily applauded. She felt so strongly about the 'impudent proposal' that she sat down at once on the very day in May 1853 that she received Ellen's account, and dashed off her impetuous 'My Dear Mr Clergyman and Mrs Clergyman', repeating later at the end of her delayed letter a month later, 'Don't go and live with Mrs Clergyman'.

LETTER 25

*Mary Taylor to Ellen Nussey, May to 21 July 1853, WS no.
856; text from MS. in Berg Collection, New York Public
Library. No postmark.*

My Dear Mr Clergyman and Mrs Clergyman
    I have received your letter expressing a wish to have my
services as companion. Your terms are so indefinite and so
low that I had rather have nothing to do with you. As I
understand your proposal you offer me board and lodging
but no clothes or means of getting any. If you intend providing my dress I shd like to know what liberty I shd have
in the choice and make and who had worn the things before
me, tho I must say this wd not alter my refusal of yr offer
as I shd still not be so well off as a servant girl. The pecuni-
ary advantages you offer at some future time I consider
worth nothing. They are quite indefinite; the time when I
am to receive them is too far off, and the condition that you
make,—that you must be dead before I can profit by them,
decides me to refuse them altogether.
    Your letter is as indefinite abt the services you require as
abt the wages you offer. As to the companionship, affection
etc I have very little to offer to a stranger—and it strikes me
I shd never have much for you. Your coarseness of feeling
that allows you to [pay] me the greater part of my wages
only after your death, your evident dishonesty in leaving
the engagement so indefinite that I might do two women's
work for twenty years to come and then have no /legal/
claim either on you or your heirs, yr evident notion that an
expensive dress and diet is to compensate for the absence
of money wages, all make me think that your feelings,
principles and pleasures are very different to mine, and there
could be no companionship in the case. As to my services I
wd not give them without certain money wages paid quar-
terly, and certain time to be at my own disposal. These are
what every servant gets, and I shd want something more.
                                            Yours.

May. Dr [dear] Ellen Here's my opinion on the impudent

proposal you mention in yr letter, which I received this morning along with one from Amelia. All yr news is very interesting, particularly that concerning Joe, Amelia, and Charlotte. My last letters told quite a contrary tale. They were none of them well and that was proved more by their low spirits than their complaints. I've no doubt Tim[1] is a little pest /as Joe says/ but that is no reason why it shd not be brought up healthy if possible. I am sorry to hear its intellect is so forward, it ought to look stupid and get fat.

June 26. I have kept my letter back because I had not said all I had to say, and now it's gone out of my head. Since then I have received a letter fm you, dated 7 Oct 52. It came along with some fm Hunsworth of 20 and 23 Feb/53, and one fm John dated 20 Oct/52. You mention Mr Brontë's illness and C. Brontë's liver complaint.[2] I had heard of them both but not from her. I did not know her liver complaint still continued, and since the date of yours I hear from Amelia that you and she have been at Hun.[3] and C.B. was very well indeed—How are you all now I wonder?

I hear I mean read that there is a box full of treasures on the way to me Per *Maori*, now at Nelson.[4] All the sailors

---

[1] 'Tim' is Emily Martha, daughter of Joseph and Amelia Taylor, b. 1851. She was a sickly child, not improved by her parents' eccentric treatment. Charlotte wrote about it in 1852: 'I don't know what that dear Mrs Joe Taylor will make of her little one in the end: between port-wine and calomel . . . I should not like to be in its socks' (WS no. 760) and 'when I read to Papa Mrs Joe Taylor's account of her system with the poor little water-patient, he said, if that child died, its parents ought to be tried for infanticide!' (WS no. 765). The child died in August 1858.

[2] Charlotte had recurrent liver attacks in 1851-52. Mr Brontë suffered a slight stroke in August 1852.

[3] Ellen's visit to Joseph and Amelia Taylor at Hunsworth is noted in Charlotte's letter of 26 October 1852 but possibly Mary refers to some visit paid during Charlotte's stay with Ellen in late November 1852 (WS nos. 791, 800-05).

[4] The *Maori* arrived at Nelson from London on 8 June, and at Wellington on 21 July, but the local papers make no mention of these troubles.

have run away—very sensible of them when they are probably pd [paid] £2 a month and by keeping out of sight till the *Maori* is gone can hire themselves here for £7.—They— I don't mean the sailors—have got some Maories to land the cargo, but as they can't persuade them to go up aloft there is no knowing when the ship can come on here.

Well; in the said box is a pair of lace cuffs from you for me to wear "when I go to a dance." Do you think I go once a week to a dance? I am very curious to see them and particularly to know if the fashion of them is still unknown here—in which case they will certainly set me up for a twelvemonth. It is a great mercy and a particular favour of Providence that they were not sent in the *Mahomet Shah.*[5]

I go to a dance now and then. I get an invitation from somebody in the name of some *"party"* or parties unknown. We dance at the Hall of the Athenaeum hired and decorated with flags and green stuff for the occasion. We muster about 25 couple, dance with great gravity and call ourselves *very select*. The thing is managed by some second and third rate bachelors who don't know how to give their invites properly in a body, and individually had rather not *"come forward."*

My best amusement is to put on a hood—such as children wear and very common here for grown people—and go after I've shut up at night, and gossip with a neighbour. I have 4 or five houses where I do this and talk more *real talk* in an hour than in all the nigh[t] at a dance.

July 2. I have just found out it was not you but Amelia that sent me the lace cuffs, and you and C.B. concocted the rest of the box. I have no doubt I shall approve of yr choice as A. says. Were you all together in the little room at Hunsworth? Giving her yr advice—Mind if the dress is scarlet or pale green I'll never forgive you.

I folded this letter once without putting my name to [it]. Wellington July 21/53. Don't go and live with Mrs Clergyman.

M. Taylor

[5] Destroyed by fire off the Australian coast on 19 April 1853.

Meanwhile, in Haworth on 13 December 1852, the Rev. Arthur Nicholls, her father's curate, proposed to Charlotte. She refused him, but the irrational fury of old Mr Brontë at the very idea of such a thing undoubtedly turned the scales in Mr Nicholls's favour. Something of this was told to Mary by Ellen, to judge by Mary's remarks in February 1854.

LETTER 26

Mary Taylor to Ellen Nussey, 24 February to 3 March 1854, WS no. 879; text from MS. in Ashley Collection, British Museum. No postmark.

Feb. 24/54

Dear Ellen

I got a letter from you some time ago Pr [per] Constantine[1] dated Brookroyd Aug 12/53 just abt six months ago. I thank you for your trouble concerning my dress and bonnet. You may have the satisfaction of knowing it was not in vain, as they both turned out wonderfully well, and I shall certainly accept yr kind offer and get another in time for next winter but one. How ever did you manage to make the dress so heavy? and then call it not a winter dress! It fitted well, tho it was too long; a very small fault. The bonnet just suited me. The thermometer just now rises to abt 80° every day wherefore the fine things are put by. I shall bring them out in due time. You cannot imagine the importance they give me. The peak behind is the object of universal admiration.

I am glad you approved of my lecture to Joe on diet, tho' you are mistaken in thinking that I follow my own advice. In summer I never eat 6 dinners in the week, seldom more than three. My health suffers less from low living than it wd from biliousness were I to eat more. Luckily winter comes, and I can keep up my strength and have an easy mind and clear head at the same time. I seldom taste anything stronger than tea either in hot weather or cold.

[1] Arrived at Wellington from London on 4 February 1854.

You talk wonderful nonsense abt C. Brontë in yr letter.[2]
What do you mean about "bearing her position so long, and
enduring to the end"? and still better—"bearing our lot
whatever it is". If its C's lot to be married shd n't she bear
that too? or does your strange morality mean that she shd
refuse to ameliorate her lot when it lies in her power. How
wd she be inconsistent with herself in marrying? Because
she considers her own pleasure? If this is so new for her to
do, it is high time she began to make it more common. It
is an outrageous exaction to expect her to give up her
choice in a matter so important, and I think her to blame in
having been hitherto so yielding that her friends can think
of making such an impudent demand.—Yr account of yr
trip to Yarmouth[3] is amusing. I am right glad you came back
again.

All your gossip is very interesting. Mrs Joe Taylor sends
me very little being used I think to spend her time too much
at home. Perhaps when her health improves, she will take
more interest in her neighbours.

I wish you could see how busy I am *going to be*. I have
got such a lot of things coming! Finery of all kinds. It will
take me a fortnight's hard work to get them all arranged
and ticketed. And then the people that will come to see
them! I always find myself wondering at these people with
one eye while I wait on them with the other. It gives them
such evident pain to see anything they can't buy, and it is so
impossible for not[4] to look at the most expensive things, even
when they can't buy any but the cheapest. Then the tricks
they play on their husbands' head or heart or purse, to get

---

[2] Ellen's letter of 12 August 1853 has told Mary of Mr Nicholls's
proposal to Charlotte, about which Charlotte wrote to EN in
letters of 15 December 1852, and in 1853 on 2 January, 4 March,
6 April, 16, 19, and 27 May. At the stage at which Ellen wrote to
Mary, Mr Nicholls had left Haworth (27 May), and he did not
return until January 1854, although he and Charlotte corresponded
in the autumn of 1853.

[3] Ellen passed through Yarmouth on her way to the Upjohns at
Gorleston, in May 1853.

[4] Thus in MS.

the money! And then the coolness with [which] they'll say they don't care a bit about it only thought they might as well have it! There are some silk mantles coming about which more lies will be told than would make a lawyer's fortune; to me, their husbands' friends and neighbours. Don't think all my customers answer to this description. Yet it's wonderful how many do.

I've got an addition to my store by which you may see I'm getting on in the world.[5] It has 20 feet frontage and is 16 ft deep. So that my house now looks like I could let it for £50 or £60 Pr an. [per annum] but then the ground is not paid for.
I intend to pay for it this winter. My coming home seems just as far off as ever; that is two or three years more. In that time I expect this town and colony to advance wonderfully. There will be steam communication via Panama[6]—perhaps I'll come home that way. There will be a large export of wool to England and kai[7]—provisions, to Australia. Then there are signs of a mania for emigration to N. Zealand coming on—a sort of fever which will injure those who get it, but will benefit the colony generally. Old settlers of course encourage this mania as it is to their own advantage. Indeed so long as people come of their judgement there is no doubt they will do well. Labouring men get six shillings a day and every other kind of work is paid in proportion. But once let it be understood that a man can get rich just by coming here and we shall have such cargoes of helpless silly people!

There were a family of that kind came here once and settled in the country. They brought a man servant for the gentleman and a maid for the lady and a few more servants. They went into the country about two day's journey from Wellington after making themselves remarkable for awhile in the town with their extraordinary ringlets, ribbons fly

5 Mary's sketch of her new facade may be compared with the photograph of 1866, Plate 5.
6 This project was much discussed at this date, partly because of the need for quicker access to the Californian goldfields, as well as to Australia and New Zealand.
7 'Kai' is Maori for 'food'.

away hats and frippery of all kinds. After a few months I heard they were in great distress—nearly starving. All their servants had left them, and they were all ill in bed. "Why what's the matter with them?" "Oh the musquitoes have bitten them so!"

I wish you would send me some more particular account of yourself in your next letter. You write twice a year and I quite lose the thread of your wanderings between the letters. One newspaper sent me is addressed to you at *Oundle* vicarage. Where in the world is *Oundle*?[8] And what have you been doing there? You appear to travel about a good deal. When I see you again you will have travelled much more than I have, though people won't think so. You don't mention Miss Wooler.[9] Have you seen her or rather do you see her when you come home from your peregrinations?

Good bye dear Ellen I have written to the last minute. Yours affectionately Mary Taylor.   Mar 3d/54

Nicholls left Haworth in May 1853, but a correspondence was maintained, and in January 1854 he began to wear down the opposition to the marriage. Mr Brontë capitulated when it became apparent that Nicholls would resume his Haworth curacy, and that Charlotte would still live 'at home'. On 11 April 1854 she told Ellen of their engagement, and she was married on 29 June. Ellen went to the wedding, as did Miss Wooler, who at the last moment gave Charlotte away, when Mr Brontë turned recalcitrant and refused to attend. By the time that Mary's next letter was written, Mr and Mrs Nicholls had been for their honeymoon in Ireland and were back in the parsonage at Haworth.

[8] Ellen visited her brother, Rev. Joshua Nussey, at Oundle, North-amptonshire, in June 1853, immediately following her flight from the Upjohns (WS nos. 854, 855).

[9] Miss Wooler lived for some years at the Vicarage, Heckmond-wike, not far from Birstall, with her brother-in-law, the Rev. E. N. Carter (WS no. 816, etc.).

LETTER 27

Mary Taylor to Ellen Nussey, 10 August 1854, WS no. 911; text from MS. in Ashley Collection, British Museum. Postmarked at Leeds 15 December 1854.

Dear Ellen,

My conscience has been reproaching me for the last month for neglecting my correspondence. I have done neither that nor anything else except what I could not shirk. Without being positively ill I have been dull and indifferent to everything but new arrivals or something equally important. I have cured myself, or at least bettered myself for the present, having a "clean down", and have just taken out a bundle that ought to have been answered long since.

I am very well content with my dresses and bonnets, and more thankful than you would think to be saved the trouble and responsibility of dressing myself. Neither of the dresses fit—it would be a wonder if they did. They are rather too expensive for my habits and make rather a contrast to my usual wear. The last bonnet fitted my face to a t, and was altogether a hit being neither too good nor too flimsy, nor too wintry nor too summery. The one before it (blue satin) I sold; it being only fit for winter and likely to last me, at the rate I should wear it, about six years.

I thank you for your information, in medical matters. It is so difficult a thing for women to get that it is a particular favour to come by any at a less expense than an illness of one's own. From Amelia's last letter I learn that you had been, or were, ill,[1] and she could not see you, being confined herself to the sofa. I am afraid myself that you have more courage than good fortune, and that your illness has not been so temporary as you hoped in your letter that it would be.

We have lately had a wonder here—viz, a steamer, Not a

---

[1] Ellen's cough is frequently mentioned in Charlotte's letters at this time.

war steamer, but a merchant vessel.[2] We thought so much
of it that the authorities agreed with the owners to hire it
for twelve months certain to ply between the N.Z. ports.
Two days ago came another wonder on the top of the first
one—another steamer walked in coming from Sydney via
Auckland. This one is likely to be a trader between here
and Australia. This last one coming in met the other going
out so we had two in sight at once, a thing that has never
happened before.

We are in general thriving—that is commercially, for as to
health the place is worse of[3] than usual. I suppose it is time
for the cholera to have come round to us, and though we
have not got it we have some change in the air or climate
which makes the place unhealthy. We have scarlatina, influ-
enza, etc. Your last letter has little news and that not lively.
I fear the confinement and dulness of illness will cast down
your spirits in spite of your good intentions. I wish this letter
could raise them for you. You are certainly better at home
when *out of* health, even when without any definite illness to
complain of—It is in this state that one feels the misery of
that service that requires you,—not to do anything, but to be
at the beck of another person, and no liberty even to be
alone. Ten hours work at breaking stones is not such a burden as this, if [you] only have the other fourteen to yourself,
with or without the "comforts of a home".

Amelia's letter speaks of little but illness—and Tim. She
calls Tim of a *forgiving disposition*. It is amusing to think of
her not venturing to vex the child for fear it should be angry,

---

[2] The *William Denny*, 595 tons, built in 1853, came from Australia
under an agreement with the Auckland Provincial Government to
run a mail service between Auckland and Sydney, timed to con-
nect with the monthly steam packet to England. The ship was in
Wellington Harbour on Wednesday 2 August, when many people
inspected her. The *Nelson*, 330 tons, was brought to New Zealand
under an agreement with the central government to run a service
between provincial ports. The conjunction of these two steamers
in the harbour on 2 August was the subject of an editorial in the
New Zealand Spectator for 5 August.

[3] Thus in MS.

and then when the baby fit of passion was over breaking out into praise of its *forgiving* disposition! Children don't forgive, they forget. And many fullgrown people who get praise for being placable are children in this respect. To forgive requires a mind full grown which does not always exist in a fullgrown body.

Wellington Aug 10/54   Mary Taylor.

Charlotte Brontë died on 31 March 1855. Mary continued however, to correspond with Ellen Nussey. By the date of the next letter Mary had been in touch with Mrs Gaskell, to whom she had sent the long letter which Charlotte had written describing the 1848 London visit (Appendix E), accompanied by a superb, full letter about their time at Roe Head, Haworth and Brussels, and indeed about all that she thought proper to record concerning her friend. A second letter followed at the end of the year. On the evidence of these letters alone one would judge that Mary had literary talent. Mrs Gaskell, recognizing their value, incorporated them bodily into the *Life*. The originals cannot be traced, but the envelope of the first letter survives among the Gaskell MSS. at Manchester University Library, where it is associated with the MS. of Charlotte's letter. It bears two postmarks from Wellington, 19 and 23 January 1856, having been delayed for the payment of extra postage. Mary's letter has been reconstructed from Mrs Gaskell's text in the first edition of the *Life*, and will be found in Appendix B. The second letter, which Mrs Gaskell mentioned in June 1857 that she had recently received (Gaskell, *Letters,* no. 348), contained, she said, many more details, which she incorporated in the third edition of the *Life*. They proved useful in filling the gaps left by the excisions which she had been forced to make under the threat of an action for libel. This second letter has also been reconstructed, and will be found in Appendix B.

Three months after she had sent off her first, overweight, packet to Mrs Gaskell, Mary wrote to Ellen.

LETTER 28

Mary Taylor to Ellen Nussey, 19 April to 10 May 1856,
WS no. 966; text from MS. in Berg Collection, New York
Public Library. Postmarked at Leeds 6 September 1856.

Apl 19/56

Dear Ellen,

I got your letter a week ago, that is 5 months after it was written. It has been the same with those from John and from Amelia. It is quite old fashioned to be so long without news from England! There were 3 mails due at once.—Your letter is most interesting concerning poor Charlotte's *life*. If for the sake of those who behaved ill to her the truth cannot be spoken, still people should not tell lies. The fact reached me even here that Mr Brontë did not chuse his daughter should marry—she wrote to me that she once dismissed Mr Nichols[1] because he (papa) was so angry that she was frightened,—frightened for *him*. It was long after, years I think that she told him that she had determined to see Mr N. again, and without positively saying yes to retract her refusal. I can never think without gloomy anger of Charlotte's sacrifices to the selfish old man—how well we know that, had she left him entirely and succeeded in gaining wealth and name and influence she would have had all the world lauding her to the skies for any trivial act of generosity that wd cost her nothing! But how on earth is all this to be set straight! Mrs Gaskell seems far too able a woman to put her head into such a wasp nest as she wd raise about her by speaking the truth of living people.[2] How she will get through with it I can't imagine. Charlotte once wrote to me

---

[1] Thus in MS. Cf Ellen Nussey in a letter of 1876: 'that villianous [sic] old Mr Brontë . . . . The old villian! . . . . Mary Taylor spoke of him as "that wicked old man".' (quoted Hopkins, p. 169).

[2] This, of course, is just what Mrs Gaskell *did* do, and she had to withdraw material from the 3rd edition, and apologise (WS no. 974). Ellen told Mrs Gaskell of Mary's remark (Gaskell, *Letters,* no. 344).

that Miss Martineau had no bump of secretiveness at all and that she (Charlotte) had dropped her acquaintance on that account. I am very curious about Miss Martineau's life. What do you mean about her having written it—is it published? Otherwise how do you know what she has said of Charlotte?[3]

Your account of Joe and Amelia agrees with the impression Amelia's letters give me. She writes late at night and seems to have spent her time nursing until every other idea has gone out of her head. She gives no news, mentions no friends, and seems to know nothing but how unhappy she is. This want of power to turn her thoughts abroad shews more depression than she herself is aware of. But what remedy? No one can take her place even if they had authority to send her away. Her very mind gets warped by the constant strain on it. I begin now to incline to John's opinion that Joe's hopelessness is a symptom of his disorder and not to be believed in. John seems to think he will get better by slow degrees.[4]

We have been in great danger of a terrible misfortune here. A fire broke out in a lot of warehouses at 2 o'clock in the morning a week ago (3rd May) and was not subdued till five.[5] It was so calm (a most unusual thing) that the smoke and flame rose perpendicularly. If there had been any wind at all, all our end of the town must have been burnt. We roof our houses with thin pieces of wood put on like slates and a slight breeze would have set a dozen roofs on fire at once. Waring's place is about 200 yds off; mine 300 yds more, but

[3] Harriet Martineau's biographical article in the *Daily News*, April 1855, is quoted by WS, IV, pp. 179-184.

[4] Joseph Taylor died of 'general debility and obstruction of the liver' on 23 March 1857, at Ilkley.

[5] On Sunday 27 April a fire which broke out 'at the head of the Bay adjoining the Custom House' destroyed the whole block of buildings about Farish Street. The *New Zealand Spectator* (30 April) mentions the providential absence of wind, and the 'high brick wall forming the south side of Messrs Hervey's Stores', which prevented total disaster. Among those who manned the buckets were Captain Rhodes and the Rev. Jonas Woodward.

there are wooden buildings all the way and I should only have had the favor of being burnt last. In 3 hours the fire destroyed the value of £15,000 and then we were much indebted to a brick wall, the only one about the whole clump of buildings, that delayed the fire a little and gave the engines power over it. Twelve years ago there was a fire and a raging wind, and buildings as distant as mine were set on fire by the sparks and embers. Nearly the whole town was burnt.[6]

Du reste I am plodding on as usual. I have good health ⟨···⟩ pleasant times though no *great* pleasures, yet little unhappiness except the recollection that I am getting old and shall soon be solitary for my friends are slipping away. I cannot say I make no new ones but some how I dont believe in them. I suppose I get selfish and suspicious. I suppose you know that in the last 18 months I have not prospered in wealth being just where I was in that respect a year and a half ago. I have no right to call this a misfortune but having been improving several years before made me unreasonable. I do not work hard enough to justify me in expectations of getting rich. Just now I have more to do and probably shall have. I wish I could set the world right on many points but above all respecting Charlotte. It would do said world good to know her and be forced to revere her in spite of their contempt for poverty and helplessness. No one ever gave up more than she did and with full consciousness of what she sacrificed. I don't think myself that women are justified in sacrificing themselves for others,[7] but since the world generally expects it of them they should at least acknowledge it. But where much is given we are all wonderfully given to gra[sp] at more. If Charlotte had left home and made a favor of returning she wd have got thanks instead of tyranny

[6] Probably Mary is referring to the fire of November 1842, which destroyed fifty-seven houses along Lambton Quay.

[7] This was not Charlotte's view. In July 1846 she advised Ellen to stay at home to mind her aged mother, because 'the right path is that which necessitates the greatest sacrifice of self-interest' (WS no. 257). Mary expressed her views fully in her articles *The First Duty of Women*.

Plate 4

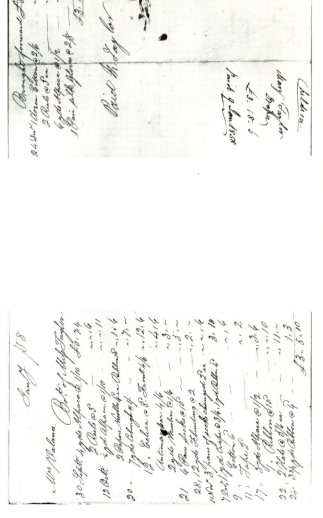

Mary Taylor's account to C. A. Vallance, January 1858

Plate 5

Mary Taylor's shop, 1866, taken from Cuba Street

—wherefore take care of yourself Ell[en] and if you chose to give a small modicum of attention to other people, *grumble hard*. Yours affectly

Mary Taylor.
Wellington May10/56

It seems that Ellen had been helping with the selection of goods for despatch to New Zealand.

LETTER 29

Mary Taylor to Ellen Nussey, 4 to 8 January 1857, WS no. 977; text from MS. in Berg Collection, New York Public Library. No postmark.

Jany 4/57

Dear Ellen

A few days ago I got a letter from you dated 2nd May/56 along with some patterns and fashion book. They seem to have been lost somehow as the box ought to have come by the Hastings and only now makes its appearance by the Philip Lang.[1] It has come very à propos for a new year's gift and the patterns were not opened twenty four hours before a silk cape was cut out by one of them. I think I made a very impertinent request when I asked you to give yourself so much trouble. I thought you would just look out a few paper patterns which you might happen to have. Your being from home made the matter give you still more trouble. The poor woman for whom I wanted them is now our first rate dressmaker. Her drunken husband, who was her main misfortune having taken himself off and not been heard off[2] lately. Your account of Joe and Amelia like all that I get of them is very melancholy—more melancholy than illness

---

[1] The *Hastings* arrived on 14 October, and the *Philip Laing* on 24 December 1856.

[2] Thus in MS.

even. It seems to shew them absorbed in themselves and their misfortunes so as to shut other people out by their own miseries. That Amelia should want to keep Tim's[3] affection all to herself I can well imagine. I often see the feeling here especially where there is only one child. It needs to have half a dozen and plenty to do, for the Mama to find out that she may as well let any one love the children who will take the trouble even if the children should love them in return. Poor Amelia has a hard life of it for her one hope is so delicate and the care they take of it is so little successful in its results that I am afraid there is more pain than pleasure on the whole.

I am glad to hear that Mrs Gaskell is progressing with the *life*. I wish I had kept Charlotte's letters now though I never felt it safe to do so until latterly that I have had a home of my own. They would have been much better evidence than my imperfect recollection and infinitely more interesting. A settled opinion is very likely to look absurd unless you give the grounds for it and even if I could remember them it looks as if there might be other facts which I have neglected which ought to have altered it.— Your news of the "neighbours" is very interesting; especially of Miss Wooler and my old schoolfellows. Why on earth has Susan Ledgard had an attack of paralysis? She is still in the thirties.[4] There must have been some strong cause for it. Was it mental or bodily?—I wish I knew how to give you some account of my ways and doings here and the effect of my position on me. First of all it agrees with me. I am in better health than at any time since I left school. This difference wont seem much to other people since I never was *ill* since then; but it is very great to me for it is just the difference between everything being a burden and everything being more or less a pleasure. Half from physical weakness and half from depression of spirits my judgement in former

---

[3] i.e., her child Emily Martha, now aged five.

[4] Probably Susan Armitage Ledgard, d. of Daniel and Catherine Ledgard, who was christened on 11 May 1820 at Mirfield (Parish Register). She was a fellow pupil at Roe Head, and is mentioned in Martha Taylor's letter of May 1832, given in Appendix C.

days was always at war with my will. There was always plenty to do but never anything that I really felt was worth the labour of doing. My life now is not overburdened with work, and what I do has interest and attraction in it. I should think it is that part that I shall think most agreeable when I look back on my death bed—a number of small pleasures scattered over my way, that, when seen from a distance will seem to cover it thick.—They don't cover it by any means, but I never had so many.

I look after my shopwoman; make out bills;[5] decide who shall have "trust" and who not. Then I go a buying; not near such an anxious piece of business now that I understand my trade and have moreover a good "credit". I read a good deal; sometimes on the sofa; a vice I am much given to in hot weather. Then I have some friends. Not many and no geniuses.—Which fact pray keep strictly to yourself for the doings[6] and sayings of Wellington people in England always come out again to N.Z. I do not think my acquaintances are inferior to what I should have had elsewhere even with more means and a higher position of my own. They are most of them narrow minded and ignorant. Those of the higher class only differ by being less practical and more exacting. They are not very interesting any way. This is my fault in part for I can't take interest in their concerns. It would be dreadful to me to spend as much time as they do on the details of dressing and eating—at least providing the eating. Then their children of course concern me but little.—A book is worth any of them and a good book worth them put together. Mamas included.

Our place is thriving on the whole though there is an attempt making just now to get up a rage for emigrating and exporting to N. Zealand. Such rages always go too far and we shall likely get a bad character among you in consequence.—It's all the same to us—I wish I had better news of your own health. I think pain in the chest a serious thing.

---

[5] Mary's shopwoman was Miss M. Smith. Some of Mary's bills survive, including one made out to the tenant of her house, C. A. Vallance (Vallance journal, in Levin & Co. Papers, MS., A.T.L.) See Plate 4.

[6] The MS. reads 'for hear the doings'.

Our East winds are much the pleasantest and healthiest we
have—The soft moist northwest brings headache and depression—it even blights the trees.

Yours affectionately

Mary Taylor

Jany. 8/57

Mary's thoughts were now turning homewards, as is indi-
cated by a remark in a letter from Miss Wooler to Ellen in
the autumn of 1857 (WS no. 992). Meanwhile, the *Life of
Charlotte Brontë* appeared. Ellen had read it in draft in
October 1856 while visiting Mrs Gaskell in Manchester
(WS no. 975), and she read the final version in January
1857, again while on a visit to the Gaskells (Shaen, p. 167).
She 'approved of it altogether'. It was published in February,
when Mrs Gaskell at once had a copy sent off to Mary in
New Zealand (Gaskell, *Letters,* no. 344).

Mary acknowledged the receipt of the book in July.

LETTER 30

*Mary Taylor to Mrs Gaskell, 30 July 1857; text from WS
no. 987.*

Wellington, 30th July, 1857.

My Dear Mrs Gaskell,—I am unaccountably in receipt by
post of two vols containing the 'Life of C. Brontë.' I have
pleasure in attributing this compliment to you; I beg, therefore, to thank you for them. The book is a perfect success,[1]
in giving a true picture of a melancholy life, and you have
practically answered my puzzle as to how you would give an
account of her, not being at liberty to give a true description

---

[1] The Rev. Patrick Brontë also thought well of the *Life,* though
objecting to some details of his own portrait. 'It is in every way
worthy of what one great Woman should have written of Another,
. . . it ought to stand, and will stand, in the first rank of Bio-
graphies till the end of time' (Lock, pp. 508-9).

of those around. Though not so gloomy as the truth, it is perhaps as much so as people will accept without calling it exaggerated, and feeling the desire to doubt and contradict it. I have seen two reviews of it. One of them sums it up as 'a life of poverty and self-suppression,' the other has nothing to the purpose at all. Neither of them seems to think it a strange or wrong state of things that a woman of first-rate talents, industry, and integrity should live all her life in a walking nightmare of 'poverty and self-suppression.' I doubt whether any of them will.

It must upset most people's notions of beauty to be told that the portrait at the beginning is that of an ugly woman.[2] I do not altogether like the idea of publishing a flattered likeness. I had rather the mouth and eyes had been nearer together, and shown the veritable square face and large disproportionate nose.

I had the impression that Cartwright's mill was burnt in 1820, not in 1812.[3] You give much too favourable an account of the black-coated and Tory savages that kept the people down, and provoked excesses in those days. Old Roberson[4] said he 'would wade to the knees in blood rather than the then state of things should be altered,'—a state including Corn law, Test law, and a host of other oppressions.

Once more I thank you for the book—the first copy, I believe, that arrived in New Zealand.—Sincerely yours,

Mary Taylor

---

[2] The 1st edition of the *Life* carried an engraving of George Richmond's portrait of Charlotte. Mrs Gaskell described her features as 'plain, large, and ill-set', with a 'crooked mouth and large nose', but added that 'the eyes and the power of the countenance overbalanced every physical defect' (p. 94).

[3] The attack on the mill in *Shirley* was based on the Luddite attack on William Cartwright's mill, Rawfold's Mill at Liversedge, on 11 April 1812. An attempt to murder Cartwright was made on 18 April (Wroot ; Lock).

[4] Rev. Hammond Roberson, who opposed the Luddites (Cadman ; Wroot ; Lock). C. K. Shorter's 1896 text in *Charlotte Brontë and Her Circle* gives the spelling 'Robertson', which was probably Mary's.

As a result of her endeavour to speak the truth, Mrs Gaskell and Smith Elder her publishers were plunged into immediate trouble, and had to withdraw material and issue a public apology. When Mary heard of all this, she wrote to Ellen as follows.

LETTER 31

Mary Taylor to Ellen Nussey, 28 January 1858; text from WS no. 994.

January 28th, 1858.

Dear Ellen,—Your account of Mrs Gaskell's book was very interesting. She seems a hasty, impulsive person, and the needful drawing back after her warmth gives her an inconsistent look. Yet I doubt not her book will be of great use. You must be aware that many strange notions as to the kind of person Charlotte really was will be done away with by a knowledge of the true facts of her life. I have heard imperfectly of farther printing on the subject. As to the mutilated edition that is to come, I am sorry for it.[1] Libellous or not, the first edition was all true, and except the declamation all, in my opinion, useful to be published.[2] Of course I don't know how far necessity may make Mrs Gaskell give them up. You know one dare not always say the world moves.—Yours affectionately,

Mary Taylor.

The last of the New Zealand letters that survives is this, written to Ellen in June 1858.

---

[1] The 3rd edition. The passages which were withdrawn are given in *BST*, Vol. 6 no. 31, 1921, pp. 50-64. See also the account in WS IV, pp. 214-8.

[2] Probably Mary refers to the outburst about Branwell and Mrs Robinson at p. 328 of the first volume; it followed the words 'every member of the family' at p. 289 of the Haworth edition, 1900.

LETTER 32

Mary Taylor to Ellen Nussey, 4 June 1858, WS no. 997;
text from MS. in Berg Collection, New York Public Library.
Wellington postmark 5 June 1858.

Dear Ellen   Wellington. June 4/58
    I have lately heard through Amelia that you have lost
your Mother and that you are leaving Brookroyd.[1] Where
to? And how will you be situated? I imagine you now with
plenty of leisure and independence but with a sense of deso-
lation arising from the strange place you are in and even
from the want of your accustomed work and anxiety. — I
shall not ever see Brookroyd again and one of the people
who lived there and one whom I used to see there I shall
never see more. Keep yourself well dear Ellen and gather
round you as much happiness and interest as you can, and
let me find you cheery and thriving when I come.—When
that will be I don't yet know; but one thing is sure. I have
given over ordering goods from England so that I must
sometime give over for want of anything to sell. The last
things ordered I expect to arrive about the beginning of the
year 1859. In the course of that year therefore I shall be
left without anything to do or motive for staying. Possibly
this time twelvemonth I may be leaving Wellington.[2] Amelia
writes that Tim has got her last tooth through so that I suppose the danger is over. Certainly Amelia's life does not
impress me favourably as to the happiness of even a suitable
marriage. I think (my choice being free) that I would
rather not have my all of earthly pleasure hang on so slender
a thread though it might be that my enjoyment were less
intense. The absorption of her letters make[3] one tremble for

---

[1] After Mrs Nussey's death in December 1857, Ellen went to live
   at Laneside House, Birstall, with her sisters, Mercy Nussey and
   the widowed Ann Clapham.
[2] Mary left Wellington for Wanganui on the coastal vessel *Seagull*
   on 20 May 1859. The date of her final departure from New Zealand is not known.
[3] Thus in MS.

her. I can well imagine that she will gradually drop all her
friends out of sheer forgetfulness and be quite unconscious
of her selfishness owing to the disguise it takes. I should not
like to be the one to advise her to think now and then of
something else for were the poor thing to die she would
certainly think it had got its mortal injury in the time she
was not thinking of it.[4]

We are here in the height of a political crisis.[5] The election for the highest office in the province, (Superintendent)
comes off in about a fortnight. Moreover we have just got
a judge landed, for the first time these two years, and one
of the members of our provincial council has been waiting
for the Supreme court to sit to go to law with the late Superintendent who is also a candidate for re-election. There is

---

[4] Emily Martha Taylor, aged six, died of dysentery on 24 August
1858.

[5] A lively account of all this is given by C. R. Carter, in his *Life
and Recollections of a New Zealand Colonist,* 1866. Dr Featherston, Superintendent of the Province, had resigned in April but
refused to give up executive powers to the Speaker, Alfred Ludlam. Wellington had been without a Supreme Court Judge since
Mr Justice Stephen's departure in 1855, but Mr Justice Gresson
arrived on circuit in 1858. A special case was put to him at a
Civil Sitting to determine the issue between Featherston and
Ludlam, and he ruled on 12 June that 'the plaintiff, as Speaker
of the Provincial Council, is the proper person to perform and
exercise the executive powers of the Superintendent'. Featherston's supporters then resigned in a body.
Nomination day was 14 June. Waring Taylor was personally
involved, being Chairman of Featherston's Committee. 'I had
never before seen so much agitation and enthusiasm ;' writes
Carter. 'The Featherston party . . . . issued printed statistical
statements and witty squibs on coloured placards ; they had their
poet to sing their own praises, and cover their opponents with
ridicule' (p. 139). Featherston's election colours were red, white
and blue ; presumably Mary sold only these ribbons, but the
opponents sported green and white. 'Scores of pounds were ex-
pended in ribbons, in silks, in calicoes, and woollen stuffs of the
right colors ; the stocks of the drapers ran short' (p. 142). Because
the nominations did not give a clear decision, a poll was de-
manded, held on 28 June, when Featherston was re-elected.
Waring Taylor's later political career is outlined in *DNZB*.

altogether a small storm going on in our teacup, quite brisk enough to stir everything in it. My principal interest therein is the sale of election ribbons; though I am afraid owing to the bad weather there will be little display.—Besides the elections there is nothing interesting. We all go on pretty well. I have got a pony about four feet high that carries me about ten miles from Wellington which is much more than walking distance, to which I have been confined for the last ten years. I have given over most of the work to Miss Smith who will finally take the business,[6] and if we had finer weather I think I should enjoy myself. We have a very wet and early winter and have had no earthquakes for a long time which is always thought a bad sign. People expect a sharp one when one comes after a long interval of quiet.— My main want here is for books enough to fill up my idle time. It seems to me that when I get home I will spend half my income on books, and sell them when I have read them, to make it go farther. I know this is absurd, but people with an unsatisfied appetite think they can eat enormously. It rains just now five days out of six.

Remember me kindly to Miss Wooler and tell me more about her in your next. You must by no means give over writing to me until I tell you. If I dont sail till next year at this time you may safely write until April i.e. by the March mail. Fill your letters with gossip. You are mistak[en] in thinking I hear much. Amelia ⟨···⟩ me.[7] Describe y[our] new dwelling and employments. I cant [think] where you will go or what you will do, Without ⟨···⟩ al work. Write quickly and fully and tell me all about i[t affec]tionately

Mary Taylor

Mary left Wellington for Wanganui on the coastal vessel *Seagull* on 20 May 1859, on the first stage no doubt of that 'hallack' about New Zealand which she had promised herself in 1848. Waring Taylor had estates in the Rangitikei district (for which Wanganui was a port of access), while

[6] See Introduction to Part III.
[7] The page is mutilated here.

his brother-in-law, Robert John Knox, was managing estates
there for Captain W. B. Rhodes. This may well account for
Mary's setting off in that direction. By the next year she
was back in Yorkshire, where she lived for the rest of her
life in a house built for her at Gomersal, to which she gave
the name High Royd. One letter has been found dating after
her return. It was written in 1863 to the invaluable Ellen
Nussey.

LETTER 33

*Mary Taylor to Ellen Nussey, probably 1863, not previously
published; text from MS. in Berg Collection, New York
Public Library.*

Dear Ellen

Mrs Battye never came on account of Lizzie being—not
poorly very, but too ailing to be left alone and there was no
servant housekeeper or help to leave her with.[1] Mr Battye
came at 7 or 8 o'clock and played whist with me Mrs Taylor
and Tom.[2] I heard the Carr's had a relation (Lady Audrey)
coming on a visit and so never asked them.[3] There were
plenty of people at Mrs Booth's[4]—80 I suppose, dancing in

[1] John Battye, solicitor, of Birstall, in 1854 married Hannah Cockill
(see Table D). Their only child, Elizabeth Hannah Battye, b.
1856, must be 'Lizzie'.

[2] Mrs Jane Lister Taylor, née Charlesworth, wife of Mary's eldest
brother Joshua (III), and her son Thomas Charlesworth Taylor
(1842-1900). See Table A.

[3] The family of Charles Carr, solicitor, of Hill Top, Gomersal.
Grace, wife of Charles Carr senior, died on 22 October 1863,
aged 88. Either of her two daughters, Anne or Elizabeth, could
be Mary's 'Miss Carr'. Mrs Charles Carr junior, née Eleanor
Walker, was sister to Mary, wife of Ellen's brother John. See
Tables C and E. Her daughter married Rev. William Margetson
Heald in 1844 (see Letter 11). Lady Audrey is not traced.

[4] Mrs Mary Booth, née Sigston (d. 1883), widow of Dr James
Booth, and mother of Ann Elizabeth Taylor, wife of Mary's
eldest nephew Joshua (IV). She lived at Gomersal Old Hall.
There were several other daughters. The Booths were related to
both Nusseys and Taylors in the grandparents' generation.

one room and talking in another. I did not stay supper but Mrs Booth took me into the kitchen to direct telling her daughters that she thought I should like it as I "had not had much opportunity of seeing things in that style." The dishes were very nice but all crowded together from the necessity of entertaining so many. I talked to Miss Taylor[5] a good while. She looked tired.

The very day that Miss Carr and the Healds left Mrs Carr was taken ill with some thing almost like a fit.[3] She had leeches behind the ears and remains in an exceedingly weak state. She is 86 years old.—I am sorry you were so ill before you went because of course the journey knocked you up and will deprive you of the benefit of the change.

Who is the Mr Campbell who was drowned with his family in New Zealand? I have not seen the account. Where did it happen?[6]

Give my love to Miss Wooler and tell her I saw two Miss Carters[7] at Mrs Booth's. They looked very nice, and appeared to enjoy themselves. My nephews have all learned to dance in some clandestine way,[8] and danced till 2 o'clock. Their mother took it very patiently and seemed to enjoy it. If there is a library at Hornsea[9] get Mendelsohn's letters from Italy, also Olmstead's American Slave States,[10] and some others of his. I should like to subscribe to Mudie's

---

[5] One of the Taylors of Purlwell Hall, Batley, relations of Ellen's. See Table C, and Nussey, *BST,* vol. 15 no. 4, 1969, pp. 331-6.

[6] Not traced.

[7] Miss Wooler's nieces, Susan and Kate, who later conducted a school at Oakwell Hall ; see *BST,* 1969, p. 309 for a note on poor Miss S. Carter's later misadventure.

[8] Since Mary's brother Joshua (III) and his wife belonged to the Moravian Church at Gomersal, they may have disapproved of dancing.

[9] Ellen may have been with Miss Wooler at Hornsea (*SBC,* pp. 260-2 ; *BST* vol. 12, no. 2, 1952, pp. 113-4).

[10] These are probably F. L. Olmsted's *A Journey in the Seaboard Slave States,* 1856, and Mendelssohn's *Letters from Italy and Switzerland,* translated by Lady Wallace, published in London in 1862.

for I have discontinued my subscription to the Smith Library
Co. and get no foreign books now.

I hope you will come back quite well and keep so through
the winter when you get home.

Affectionately yours
M Taylor

High Royd
    29th.

PART FOUR

Aftermath

In her Yorkshire retirement Mary Taylor, now forty-six, set about completing the writing which had occupied her for so long. The first work to be printed, on her favourite subject, 'The First Duty of Women', was a series of articles which appeared in the *Victoria Magazine* at intervals between 1865 and 1870, and was published as a book in London in 1870.

Mary states boldly that 'the object of most of the papers is to inculcate the duty of earning money'. The fourteen articles make sad reading today, as propaganda for old won causes is apt to do. They are penetrated with bitterness at the emptiness of the lives to which middle-class women were condemned if they did not marry. There is no hardship in work, asserts our experienced Mary; on the contrary, 'the greatest [hardship] of all is often staying in and doing nothing.' Women should be given the chance, in Charlotte's words (WS no. 169) of 'active exertion, a stake in life.' Mary had held this belief since girlhood, to judge by the speeches of Rose Yorke in *Shirley*.

Among other themes which Mary had long ago argued out with Ellen and Charlotte are those of womanly self-sacrifice, the hatefulness of dependence in another's house (as a governess, or unwanted sister), and that marriage is

not the only solution to women's problems. Women should
have some 'acceptable alternative', otherwise they may be
driven into matrimony merely for maintenance, or may have
to starve when the husband is gone. Let every woman learn
to *earn,* says Mary, as teacher, nurse, prison matron,—or in
a shop. Charlotte Brontë of course raised some of these
issues in *Shirley,* especially in chapter 12, and Mary also
tried to embody them in a novel. The liveliest item is 'The
Old Dispute', a dramatic dialogue between a Gentleman and
a Lady, who develop a sparkling quarrel. Needless to say,
the Lady wins the argument.

Much in these articles must have been startling in 1865-
70: the belief that 'ladies' who will not soil their hands are
of less value than labourers; that women have brains, even
for science; that submission is NOT the duty of anybody
over twenty-one, regardless of sex; that Milton's dictum
about the roles of man and woman, 'He for God only, she
for God in him', is unacceptable because Eve may not find
'God in him'. No wonder that the pious, pliant, submissive
Ellen Nussey thought the mature Mary Taylor 'peculiar'.

Five years later Mary was again in print, this time as one
of the authors of *Swiss Notes by Five Ladies,* Leeds, 1875.
She is the 'Frau Mutter', the 'originator, *chaperone,* and
moving spirit' of a ten week expedition undertaken by herself and four young women, with whom she shares the book.
One of them wrote: 'She will laugh, sing, and jodel with any
of us, and has spirit for anything the most adventurous members of the Alpine Club ever did or thought of doing; but
unfortunately lacks breath' (p. vii). That is not surprising,
since Mary by this time was nearly sixty. 'Frau Mutter'
organizes the party up Mont Blanc, and to the St Bernard
Hospice, and to Italy. She copes with language, guides, por-
ters, horses, carriages, and currency. There is one fine piece
of writing, about an experience which befell, she says, 'some
years before I took four young ladies with me to Switzerland'. It is the account of 'a walk I took alone on a glacier',
losing her way among moraines and crevasses, and vividly
evoking the terror of possible death among them (p. 104).
It is clear that she had been a constant visitor to Switzer-

land. 'The Frau Mutter is quite an institution, a season hardly being considered complete till she has made her appearance' at, for example, Pontresina, 5,900 feet up in the Ober-Engadin (p. 116).

Lastly, at the very end of her days, Mary published her novel, *Miss Miles, or, A Tale of Yorkshire Life 60 Years Ago,* London, 1890.

The '60 Years Ago' takes us back to the Taylors of the Red House, in the days when Charlotte Brontë visited there, and to the places, persons, and ideas which are the stuff of *Shirley.* Because of this, while Mary's book will not compare with Charlotte's, it has considerable interest. Had it been published in 1850, instead of 1890, and so been read in the context of Mrs Gaskell's and Charlotte's studies of women and society in the northern industrial areas, *Miss Miles* might very well have made a stir. Mary missed her moment; and by 1890, though her content was still unusual, it was not markedly new, while her technique showed up by comparison with contemporary developments as very primitive indeed.

Miss Miles is set in the West Riding of Yorkshire, in the village of 'Repton', which, with its heather-covered heights and deep little river valley crowded with mills, is clearly the area of Gomersal and Birstall. There are three heroines, if not four. The titular heroine, Sarah Miles, is the fourteen year-old daughter of a grocer in the community of working-class Dissent. His shop is at what seems to be Gomersal Hill Top, where Church Lane, leading down to Birstall, cuts into the Bradford highroad along which lies the Red House. See Plate 1.

Sarah wants to go to school, since 'knowledge is power'; moreover, she despises the life in service to 'great folks' which has turned her elder sister Jane into a toady. Sarah's aunt is not helpful; 'There's no decent way fit for you to take by which a woman can earn more than just a living' she warns discouragingly.

The second and third heroines are growing up ten miles away and in another class, in the moorland parsonage of Mr Bell. Maria Bell, his daughter, has with her a friend, Dora, and her widowed mother Mrs Wells. Mrs Wells soon marries again—frankly for 'maintenance'— and Dora goes with her to the slatternly home of the new husband, Squire Woodman. Both women degenerate quickly, although Dora revolts inwardly at 'the submission that is supposed to be the lot of women'. Mrs Bell tries to help, and urges strongly upon both Dora and Maria that 'you must earn your own living . . . hold fast to that.' Mrs Wells-Woodman then dies, leaving Dora to poverty and isolation in her hateful hovel. 'Are righteous means of helping themselves never to be found for women?' asks the author at this crisis.

Time skips along until Maria and Dora are twenty-two. Mrs Bell has died. Mr Bell now also dies. Since his savings have vanished, Maria in her turn has to leave the moorland home and go down to Repton to 'earn a living'. There her mother's brother, Mr Turner, is a mill owner, one of the 'great folks'; indeed, it is in his house that Jane Miles is in service. With something of a wrench, Mary Taylor in this way joins up the working-class and the middle-class threads of her narrative.

Maria Bell is determined to teach, for 'you know teaching is the only thing a woman can do'. But the Turners, like Mary's own brothers, are horrified that a female relative should 'go out' to work, especially in a day school.

Maria persists, and opens a small school in a nearby cottage; Sarah Miles at once attends—which brings the third narrative thread back into the pattern. Sarah is not happy, for she is ignorant, she is 'only the grocer's daughter at the corner', and she attends Chapel, not Church. Moreover, she speaks broad Yorkshire. But Maria Bell helps her to overcome some of these difficulties.

In this school venture, Maria is befriended by little old Miss Everard, whose family had owned the great house before the Turners' time, and who had been a friend of Maria's mother. She is desperately poor, having lost her money—or been cheated out of it—in ways that as an untrained spinster she cannot comprehend. She and young Maria have much to discuss about loneliness for the unmarried, and education, and work. 'Don't you think, my

Plate 6

Madame Goussaert's 'Château de Koekelberg', 1887

dear,' pleads Miss Everard, 'that women ought to learn to be taught something about business?'

Working at her school, Maria Bell finds that her 'character and disposition' have changed for the better. But Dora Wells is still immured on her lonely farmstead and writes anguished letters to Maria about her fate in the shadows. These are so reminiscent of Charlotte's surviving letters that one suspects Mary may have drawn on some of these, later destroyed, which came out to her in New Zealand (She had, after all, written half the book by 1852, according to her remarks in Letter 24.) Sarah Miles, meanwhile, develops a gift for singing, and not being a 'lady' hopes to earn a little money by it.

Mary Taylor handles these different threads quite well, but she nudges her reader's understanding too often. She seems to have had in mind a less intelligent class of reader than she judged that Charlotte wrote for in *Jane Eyre,* because she constantly interrupts 'to explain or defend' her doctrines, as she noted that Anne Brontë had done. (See Letter 16.)

The investigation of woman's lot now moves up in social scale. Mrs Dodds the Vicar's wife asks Maria Bell and Miss Everard to tea with the Turner womenfolk. The Turners snub their cousin Maria, while a young engineer Branksome is attracted to her. He is to save her at the end, obviously, but Mary, as she had admitted to Charlotte, has no idea what to do with a lover in the story.

Bad times come on. Miles's shop fails, workpeople starve, ricks burn. There are meetings and marches in Manchester, Leeds, Halifax, Bradford. Sarah, who listens to the speeches, imbibes some unfeminine Radical notions. She goes at last into service with the Turners and is useful to the author as a watcher of that household, where a mysterious visitor, the business man Thelwall, is courting Amelia Turner. But the blow falls, Thelwall forecloses, the mill shuts down, the Turners and the village of Repton alike are ruined. 'Thank God I'm not a lady,' reflects Sarah. 'They are worse off than we are if they cannot do nought to help themselves.'

In the general disaster, which affects of course Maria

Bell and Miss Everard, Branksome remains true, courting
however by letter. The Turner women quarrel bitterly in
their useless misery. Amelia wishes to 'earn', but has no
notion how to. Sarah, who has grown up grave, thoughtful
and courteous, urges Amelia to rebel against the expectations of her home and class, but Amelia, though she longs
to 'look the world in the face free from debt and dependence', has not the moral courage for such defiance.

We now return to Dora Wells. On the death of her step-
father, she walks the ten miles to Repton to seek Maria's
help, determined likewise to be independent. Her idea is to
become a professional lecturer, for she has a fine voice. Mrs
Dodds and the Church folk disapprove of anything so unfeminine and unheard of. 'The idea was new, everyone felt,
and that was sin enough . . . It clashed with the customary
conventions, and that was wicked.' But Dora wins support
from the Dissenting workers, and makes a triumphant debut
at the Mechanics' Institute.

Sarah Miles meanwhile goes on her forthright Yorkshire
way, rejecting undesirables whatever their class. Thelwall
ensnares Turner still further in shady financial deals, of
which his new partner, Samuel Sykes, suitor for Sarah, begins to have suspicions.

The finale duly arrives. Miss Everard, ejected by Turner
even from her little Lodge cottage, is rescued by Maria
Bell. Turner runs away, then returns dying in a snowstorm
to confess his wicked deeds. The money out of which he had
for so long cheated Miss Everard is repaid. 'We're noan so
much ruined as we were afore,' says Sam Sykes. 'We're free
now.' Offered the opportunity of reopening the mill to save
the town, he takes the managership, and marries Sarah.
Branksome's courtship by correspondence succeeds at last,
and he and Maria settle in to the Turner great house, now
rightfully Miss Everard's, where they all three set up a
school; a boarding school, of course. The little old spinster
revives at once, for she is 'getting like a man' she realizes,
with 'something to do'. Dora, after some vicissitudes, succeeds in earning her living as a lecturer.

In these ways the 'blessings of change and activity' fall at last upon Mary Taylor's oddly assorted heroines, Sarah, Maria, Dora, and Miss Everard; but Amelia Turner wastes away to death in the prison of her middle-class respectability.

I have summarized *Miss Miles* in this fashion because, though it is of some interest in the Brontë-Taylor story, it is a very rare book. The closeness of its relationship to Mary's own life is at once obvious; the Radical experience of her girlhood is there; the rebellion against home and the defiance of convention in her later actions are there too. So is the gospel which she learnt in person and preached to Charlotte, that single women of every class need purposeful activity as much as men do, for the good of their souls as well as of society. One remembers Charlotte's words in her letter of July 1849 to Mr Williams, her publisher's reader, who had consulted her about giving his girl Louisa the chance of an education at Queen's College, London: 'one great curse of a single female life is its dependency . . . . I wish every woman in England had also a hope and a motive' (WS no. 452).

Three of the heroines remind us of different aspects of Charlotte Brontë, while the fourth, Sarah Miles, is an original. Had she been presented to the world in the days of *Mary Barton, Shirley, North and South, Alton Locke,* or *Hard Times* she would have won a modest niche in the gallery of fame.

Mary's own judgement of her work, given to Charlotte in 1852 in Letter 24, is a just one: that her women she understood 'pretty well', but not her men, especially the lover; and that the novel was full of 'music, poverty, disputing, politics, and original views of life.' It still deserves to be looked at for these, which shine through the threadbare fabric of its narrative.

In her last years, Mary apparently withdrew into her own group of friends, among whom Ellen Nussey soon ceased to have a place. Mary disapproved of the public curiosity about the Brontës, and unlike Ellen would take no further part in satisfying it. Writing to Thomas J. Wise in November 1892, Ellen put it in this way: 'Mary Taylor the "Rose York" in *Shirley,* is living, but has always proved herself *dead* to any approach on the Brontë subject, and it is understood that long ago she destroyed her letters. She is so peculiar she might prove otherwise than helpful' (MS., Brotherton Library, Leeds).

The 'peculiarity' seems to have been part of a legend, which included the local belief that she went round her house every night with a loaded pistol, owing to her harrowing experiences in 'Australia'. Here is a version of this, recorded by a descendant of Mary's solicitors the Carrs. As a small boy he attended Gomersal Church, and there saw Miss Wooler, and 'another old lady who attended, who appealed to my childish admiration much more, not only because of a very definite moustache, but because my father, who knew her, told me that she had lived alone in Australia and there used a gun not only for sporting purposes, but for purposes of defence in that country . . . '

It is a good story, too good for one not to wish it true. Charlotte had written some fifty years earlier that Mary would 'establish her own landmarks'; this indeed she did do, even if pistolling was not her habit. She 'shut her eyes for a cold plunge' into independence, first in Germany and later in New Zealand, and, as she promised, tried when she 'came up again' to tell what it had been like. Her experiences strengthen her lifelong conviction that 'a woman who works is by that alone better than one who does not' (Letters 8, 20).

APPENDIX A

Genealogical Tables

Intermarriage over several generations linked many of the families to whom Mary Taylor refers in her letters. The following brief account should be used in conjunction with the genealogical tables noted.

(a) NUSSEY-CARR (Doctor)   Tables C and E

> Sarah Nussey (1791-1864), daughter of Joshua Nussey of White Lea, Batley, and first cousin to Ellen Nussey, married Dr William Carr of Gomersal.

(b) NUSSEY-COCKILL   Tables C and D

> Joshua Nussey of White Lea, uncle to Ellen Nussey, married Sarah Clapham; Sarah's cousin Hannah Greenfield (1784-1856) married Thomas Cockill; of their two daughters, Hannah married John Battye, while Sarah was at Roe Head school with Charlotte Brontë and Mary Taylor.

(c) NUSSEY-CARR (solicitors)   Tables C and D

> John Nussey, Royal Apothecary, Ellen's eldest brother, married his second cousin Mary Walker,

child of Richard Walker and Mary Taylor of Purlwell Hall. Her sister Eleanor married Charles Carr,
socilitor, of Hill Top, Gomersal. Thus their daughter Mary, who married W. M. Heald, was distantly
connected with Ellen Nussey. Martha, a cousin of
Mary Taylor of Purlwell Hall, married Joshua
Ingham of Blake Hall, father of the Joshua Ingham (1802-66) for whom Anne Brontë was governess in 1839. Thus Nusseys and Inghams were
distantly connected also.

(d) NUSSEY-DIXON-TAYLOR   Tables A, B, and C

Ellen Nussey was related to the Dixons, cousins of
Mary Taylor, through the marriage in 1720 of her
great-aunt Elizabeth to Joshua Dixon of Leeds,
and possibly also through the marriage of her
great-uncle John Nusse(y) to a Miss Dixon.

General works consulted, additional to those noted on the
Tables, include: Peel, Cradock, Cadman, Sheard, Whitaker,
Burke *LG*.

TABLE A   TAYLOR FAMILY TREE

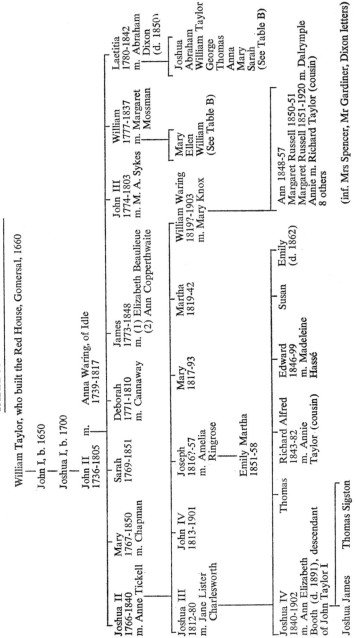

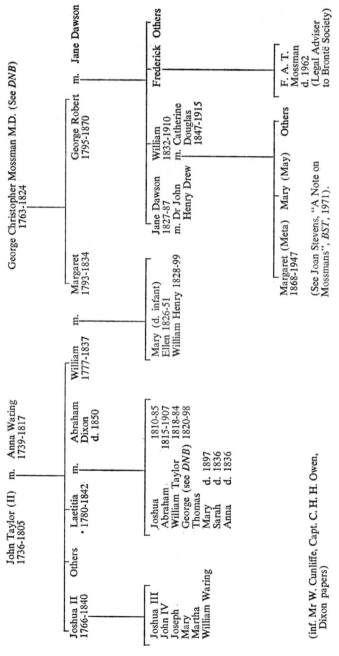

TABLE B   TAYLOR-DIXON-MOSSMAN

George Christopher Mossman M.D. (*See DNB*)
1763-1824

John Taylor (II)   m.   Anna Waring
1736-1805   1739-1817

Jane Dawson

m.   Margaret
1793-1834

George Robert
1795-1870

Frederick   Others

William
1777-1837   m.   Mary (d. infant)
                    Ellen 1826-51
                    William Henry 1828-99

Laetitia   m.   Abraham
1780-1842   Dixon
               d. 1850

Others

Joshua II
1766-1840

Jane Dawson   William
1827-87   1832-1910
m. Dr John   m. Catherine
Henry Drew   Douglas
                  1847-1915

F. A. T.
Mossman
d. 1962
(Legal Adviser
to Brontë Society)

Margaret (Meta)   Mary (May)   Others
1868-1947

(See Joan Stevens, "A Note on
Mossmans", *BST*, 1971).

Joshua   1810-85
Abraham   1815-1907
William Taylor 1818-84
George (see *DNB*) 1820-98
Thomas
Mary   d. 1897
Sarah   d. 1836
Anna   d. 1836

Joshua III
John IV
Joseph
Mary
Martha
William Waring

(inf. Mr W. Cunliffe, Capt. C. H. H. Owen,
Dixon papers)

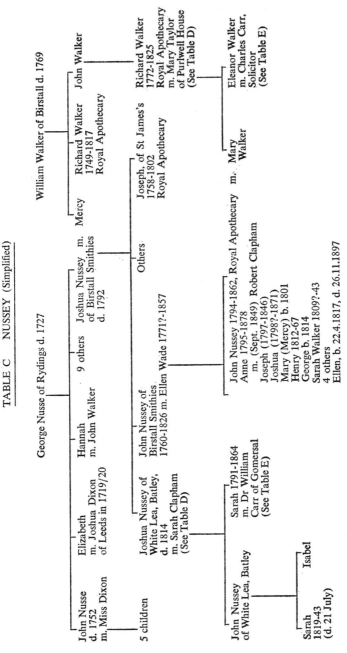

TABLE C   NUSSEY (Simplified)

(inf. Mr J. T. M. Nussey)

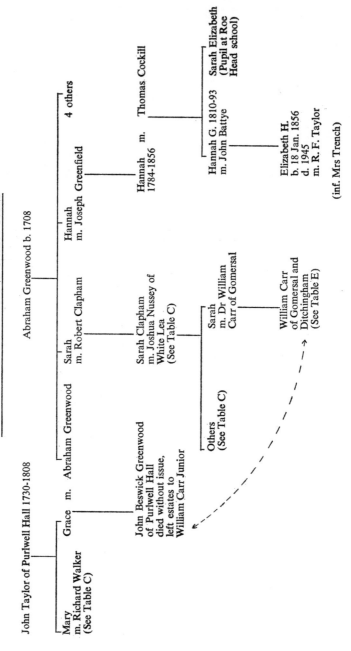

TABLE D   COCKILL-BATTYE-CARR-NUSSEY

John Taylor of Purlwell Hall 1730-1808

Abraham Greenwood b. 1708

Mary
m. Richard Walker
(See Table C)

Grace   m.   Abraham Greenwood

Sarah
m. Robert Clapham

Hannah
m. Joseph Greenfield

4 others

John Beswick Greenwood
of Purlwell Hall
died without issue,
left estates to
William Carr Junior

Sarah Clapham
m. Joshua Nussey of
White Lea
(See Table C)

Hannah   m.   Thomas Cockill
1784-1856

Others
(See Table C)

Sarah
m. Dr William
Carr of Gomersal

Hannah G. 1810-93
m. John Battye

Sarah Elizabeth
(Pupil at Roe
Head school)

William Carr
of Gomersal and
Ditchingham
(See Table E)

Elizabeth H.
b. 18 Jan. 1856
d. 1945
m. R. F. Taylor

(inf. Mrs Trench)

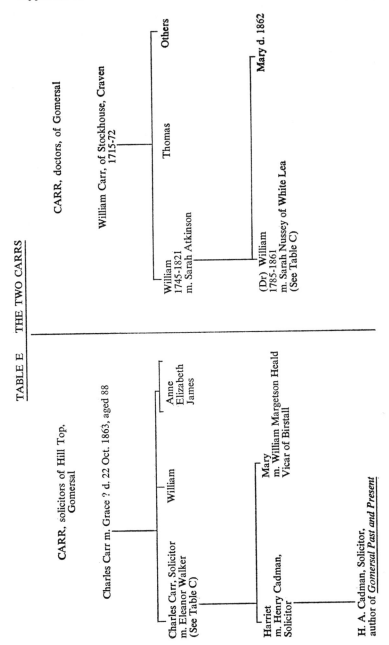

TABLE E   THE TWO CARRS

CARR, doctors, of Gomersal

William Carr, of Stockhouse, **Craven** 1715-72

Thomas   **Others**

William 1745-1821 m. Sarah Atkinson

(Dr) William 1785-1861 m. Sarah Nussey of **White Lea** (See Table C)

Mary d. 1862

CARR, solicitors of Hill Top, Gomersal

Charles Carr m. Grace ? d. 22 Oct. 1863, aged 88

William

Anne Elizabeth James

Charles Carr, Solicitor m. Eleanor Walker (See Table C)

Mary m. William Margetson Heald Vicar of Birstall

Harriet m. Henry Cadman, Solicitor

H. A. Cadman, Solicitor, author of *Gomersal Past and Present*

APPENDIX B

Mary Taylor to Mrs Gaskell, 1856

Mrs Gaskell applied to Mary Taylor for help with her *Life* of Charlotte Brontë, and received, it seems, two letters. The first, dated 18 January 1856, supplied material which was used in the first edition of the *Life,* published in February 1857. The second, to which Mrs Gaskell referred in her own letter of 3 June 1857 (*Letters,* no. 348) as recently received, provided some details which were incorporated in the third edition.

The MS. of these letters has not been located; the present text is taken from the Haworth edition of the *Life,* edited by C. K. Shorter, 1900. The extracts in the first edition came presumably from the first letter; seven more extracts were added in the third edition.

THE FIRST LETTER
(passages used in the first edition)

1. [pp. 100-1]. I first saw her coming out of a covered cart, in very old-fashioned clothes, and looking very cold and miserable. She was coming to school at Miss Wooler's. When she appeared in the schoolroom her dress was changed, but just as old. She looked a little old woman, so short-sighted that she always appeared to be seeking some-

thing, and moving her head from side to side to catch a
sight of it. She was very shy and nervous, and spoke with a
strong Irish accent. When a book was given her she dropped
her head over it till her nose nearly touched it, and when
she was told to hold her head up, up went the book after it,
still close to her nose, so that it was not possible to help
laughing.

2. [p. 101]. We thought her very ignorant, for she had never
learnt grammar at all, and very little geography.

3. [pp. 102-3]. She would confound us by knowing things that
were out of our range altogether. She was acquainted with
most of the short pieces of poetry that we had to learn by
heart: would tell us the authors, the poems they were taken
from, and sometimes repeat a page or two, and tell us the
plot. She had a habit of writing in italics (printing characters), and said she had learnt it by writing in their magazine.
They brought out a 'magazine' once a month, and wished it
to look as like print as possible. She told us a tale out of it.
No one wrote in it, and no one read it, but herself, her
brother, and two sisters. She promised to show me some of
these magazines, but retracted it afterwards, and would
never be persuaded to do so. In our play hours she sat or
stood still, with a book, if possible. Some of us once urged
her to be on our side in a game at ball. She said she had
never played, and could not play. We made her try, but soon
found that she could not see the ball, so we put her out.
She took all our proceedings with pliable indifference, and
always seemed to need a previous resolution to say "No"
to anything. She used to go and stand under the trees in the
playground, and say it was pleasanter. She endeavoured to
explain this, pointing out the shadows, the peeps of sky,
etc. We understood but little of it. She said that at Cowan
Bridge she used to stand in the burn, on a stone, to watch
the water flow by. I told her she should have gone fishing;
she said she never wanted. She always showed physical
feebleness in everything. She ate no animal food at school.
It was about this time I told her she was very ugly. Some

years afterwards I told her I thought I had been very impertinent. She replied, 'You did me a great deal of good, Polly, so don't repent of it.' She used to draw much better, and more quickly, than anything we had seen before, and knew much about celebrated pictures and painters. Whenever an opportunity offered of examining a picture or cut of any kind, she went over it piecemeal, with her eyes close to the paper, looking so long that we used to ask her 'what she saw in it.' She could always see plenty, and explained it very well. She made poetry and drawing at least exceedingly interesting to me; and then I got the habit, which I have yet, of referring mentally to her opinion on all matters of that kind, along with many more, resolving to describe such and such things to her, until I start at the recollection that I never shall.

4. [p. 103]. We used to be furious politicians, as one could hardly help being in 1832. She knew the names of the two Ministries; the one that resigned, and the one that succeeded and passed the Reform Bill. She worshipped the Duke of Wellington, but said that Sir Robert Peel was not to be trusted; he did not act from principle, like the rest, but from expediency. I, being of the furious Radical party, told her, 'How could any of them trust one another? they were all of them rascals!' Then she would launch out into praises of the Duke of Wellington, referring to his actions; which I could not contradict, as I knew nothing about him. She said she had taken interest in politics ever since she was five years old. She did not get her opinions from her father— that is, not directly—but from the papers, etc., he preferred.

5. [pp. 104-5]. She used to speak of her two elder sisters, Maria and Elizabeth, who died at Cowan Bridge. I used to believe them to have been wonders of talent and kindness. She told me, early one morning, that she had just been dreaming: she had been told that she was wanted in the drawing-room, and it was Maria and Elizabeth. I was eager for her to go on, and when she said that there was no more, I said, 'But go on! *Make it out!* I know you can!' She said

she would not; she wished she had not dreamed, for it did not go on nicely; they were changed; they had forgotten what they used to care for. They were very fashionably dressed, and began criticising the room, etc.

This habit of 'making out' interests for themselves, that most children get who have none in actual life, was very strong in her. The whole family used to 'make out' histories, and invent characters and events. I told her sometimes they were like growing potatoes in a cellar. She said, sadly, 'Yes! I know we are!'

6. [p. 140]. Three years after [the Roe Head Schooldays] I heard that she had gone as teacher to Miss Wooler's. I went to see her, and asked how she could give so much for so little money, when she could live without it. She owned that, after clothing herself and Anne, there was nothing left, though she had hoped to be able to save something. She confessed it was not brilliant, but what could she do? I had nothing to answer. She seemed to have no interest or plea-sure beyond the feeling of duty, and, when she could get the opportunity, used to sit alone and 'make out.' She told me afterwards that one evening she had sat in the dressing-room until it was quite dark, and then observing it all at once had taken sudden fright.

7. [p. 141]. From that time her imaginations became gloomy or frightful; she could not help it, nor help thinking. She could not forget the gloom, could not sleep at night, nor attend in the day.

8. [pp. 153-4]. She visited us twice or thrice when she was at Miss Wooler's. We used to dispute about politics and reli-gion. She, a Tory and clergyman's daughter, was always in a minority of one in our house of violent Dissent and Radi-calism. She used to hear over again, delivered *with authority,* all the lectures I had been used to give her at school on despotic aristocracy, mercenary priesthood, etc. She had not energy to defend herself; sometimes she owned to a *little* truth in it, but generally said nothing. Her feeble health

gave her her yielding manner, for she could never oppose any one without gathering up all her strength for the struggle. Thus she would let me advise and patronise most imperiously, sometimes picking out any grain of sense there might be in what I said, but never allowing any one materially to interfere with her independence of thought and action. Though her silence sometimes left one under the impression that she agreed when she did not, she never gave a flattering opinion, and thus her words were golden, whether for praise or blame.

9. [pp. 282-3]. When I last saw Charlotte (Jan. 1845)[1] she told me she had quite decided to stay at home. She owned she did not like it. Her health was weak. She said she would like any change at first, as she had liked Brussels at first, and she thought that there must be some possibility for some people of having a life of more variety and more communion with human kind, but she saw none for her. I told her very warmly that she ought not to stay at home; that to spend the next five years at home, in solitude and weak health, would ruin her; that she would never recover it. Such a dark shadow came over her face when I said, 'Think of what you'll be five years hence!' that I stopped, and said, 'Don't cry, Charlotte!' She did not cry, but went on walking up and down the room, and said in a little while, 'But I intend to stay, Polly.'

10. [pp. 642-3]. [Mrs Gaskell writes: I have little more to say. If my readers find that I have not said enough, I have said too much. I cannot measure or judge of such a character as hers. I cannot map out vices, and virtues, and debatable land. One who knew her long and well—the 'Mary' of this Life—writes thus of her dead friend:] She thought much of her duty, and had loftier and clearer notions of it than most people, and held fast to them with more success. It was done, it seems to me, with much more difficulty than people have of stronger nerves and better fortunes. All her

[1] It was in fact February.

life was but labour and pain; and she never threw down the
burden for the sake of present pleasure. I don't know what
use you can make of all I have said. I have written it with
the strong desire to obtain appreciation for her. Yet what
does it matter? She herself appealed to the world's judgment
for her use of some of the faculties she had—not the best,
but still the only ones she could turn to strangers' benefit.
They heartily, greedily enjoyed the fruits of her labours,
and then found out she was much to be blamed for possess-
ing such faculties. Why ask for a judgment on her from
such a world?

[After only eight more lines, Mrs Gaskell ends the *Life;* thus
she has used Mary Taylor's words as the major element in
her finale.]

THE SECOND LETTER
(extracts added in the third edition)

1. [p. 105]. Some one at school said she 'was always talking
about clever people—Johnson, Sheridan,' etc. She said,
'Now you don't know the meaning of *clever.* Sheridan might
be clever; yes, Sheridan was clever—scamps often are—but
Johnson hadn't a spark of cleverality in him.' No one appreciated the opinion; they made some trivial remarks about
'*cleverality,*' and she said no more.

This is the epitome of her life. At our house she had just
as little chance of a patient hearing, for though not school-
girlish we were more intolerant. We had a rage for practicality, and laughed all poetry to scorn. Neither she nor
we had any idea but that our opinions were the opinions
of all the *sensible* people in the world, and we used to
astonish each other at every sentence. [Mrs Gaskell's omission.] Charlotte, at school, had no plan of life beyond what
circumstances made for her. She knew that she must pro-
vide for herself, and chose her trade; at least chose to begin
it once. Her idea of self-improvement ruled her even at

school. It was to cultivate her tastes. She always said there
was enough of hard practicality and *useful* knowledge
forced on us by necessity, and that the thing most needed
was to soften and refine our minds. She picked up every
scrap of information concerning painting, sculpture, poetry,
music, etc., as if it were gold.

2. [pp. 121-2]. [I may here introduce a quotation from a letter
which I have received from 'Mary' since the publication of
the previous editions of this memoir.]

Soon after leaving school she admitted reading something
of Cobbett's. 'She did not like him,' she said; 'but all was
fish that came to her net.' At this time she wrote to me that
reading and drawing were the only amusements she had,
and that her supply of books was very small in proportion
to her wants. She never spoke of her aunt. When I saw Miss
Branwell she was a very precise person, and looked very
odd, because her dress, etc. was so utterly out of fashion.
She corrected one of us once for using the word 'spit' or
'spitting'. She made a great favourite of Branwell. She made
her nieces sew, with purpose or without, and as far as
possible discouraged any other culture. She used to keep
the girls sewing charity clothing, and maintained to me that
it was not for the good of the recipients, but of the sewers.
'It was proper for them to do it,' she said. Charlotte never
was 'in wild excitement' that I know of. When in health she
used to talk better, and indeed when in low spirits never
spoke at all. She needed her best spirits to say what was in
her heart, for at other times she had not courage. She never
gave decided opinions at such times. [Mrs Gaskell's omission.]

Charlotte said she could get on with any one who had
a bump at the top of their heads (meaning conscientious-
ness). I found that I seldom differed from her, except that
she was far too tolerant of stupid people, if they had a grain
of kindness in them.

3. [p. 141]. She told me that one night, sitting alone, about
this time, she heard a voice repeat these lines:

'Come, thou high and holy feeling,
Shine o'er mountain, flit o'er wave,
Gleam like light o'er dome and shieling.'

There were eight or ten more lines which I forget. She insisted that she had not made them, that she had heard a voice repeat them. It is possible that she had read them, and unconsciously recalled them. They are not in the volume of poems which the sisters published. She repeated a verse of Isaiah, which she said had inspired them, and which I have forgotten. Whether the lines were recollected or invented, the tale proves such habits of sedentary, monotonous solitude of thought as would have shaken a feebler mind.

4. [pp. 141-2]. Cowper's poem *The Castaway* was known to them all, and they all at times appreciated, or almost appropriated it. Charlotte told me once that Branwell had done so; and though his depression was the result of his faults, it was in no other respect different from hers. Both were not mental but physical illnesses. She was well aware of this, and would ask how that mended matters, as the feeling was there all the same, and was not removed by knowing the cause. She had a larger religious toleration than a person would have who had never questioned, and her manner of recommending religion was always that of offering comfort, not fiercely enforcing a duty. One time I mentioned that some one had asked me what religion I was of (with a view of getting me for a partisan), and that I had said that that was between God and me. Emily (who was lying on the hearthrug) exclaimed, 'That's right.' That was all I ever heard Emily say on religious subjects. Charlotte was free from religious depression when in tolerable health; when that failed, her depression returned. You have probably seen such instances. They don't get over their difficulties; they forget them when their stomach (or whatever organ it is that inflicts such misery in sedentary people) will let them. I have heard her condemn Socinianism, Calvinism, and many other 'isms' inconsistent with Church of Englandism. I used to wonder at her acquaintance with such subjects.

5. [p. 220]. [Mrs Gaskell writes, Mary's account of their journey [to Brussels] is thus given: —]
In passing through London she seemed to think our business was, and ought to be, to see all the pictures and statues we could. She knew the artists, and knew where other productions of theirs were to be found. I don't remember what we saw except St. Paul's. Emily was like her in these habits of mind, but certainly never took her opinion, but always had one to offer. [Mrs Gaskell's omission.] I don't know what Charlotte thought of Brussels. We arrived in the dark, and went next morning to our respective schools to see them. We were, of course, much preoccupied, and our prospects gloomy. Charlotte used to like the country round Brussels. 'At the top of every hill you see something.' She took long solitary walks on the occasional holidays.

6. [pp. 243-5]. The first part of her time at Brussels was not uninteresting. She spoke of new people and characters, and foreign ways of the pupils and teachers. She knew the hopes and prospects of the teachers, and mentioned one who was very anxious to marry, 'she was getting so old.' She used to get her father or brother (I forget which) to be the bearer of letters to different single men, who she thought might be persuaded to do her the favour, saying that her only resource was to become a sister of charity if her present employment failed, and that she hated the idea. Charlotte naturally looked with curiosity to people of her own condition. This woman almost frightened her. 'She declares there is nothing she can turn to, and laughs at the idea of delicacy—and she is only ten years older than I am!' I did not see the connection till she said, 'Well, Polly, I should hate being a sister of charity; I suppose that would shock some people, but I should.' I thought she would have as much feeling as a nurse as most people, and more than some. She said she did not know how people could bear the constant pressure of misery, and never to change except to a new form of it. It would be impossible to keep one's natural feelings. I promised her a better destiny than to go begging any one to marry her, or to lose her natural feelings as a

sister of charity. She said, 'My youth is leaving me; I can never do better than I have done, and I have done nothing yet.' At such times she seemed to think that most human beings were destined by the pressure of worldly interests to lose one faculty and feeling after another 'till they went dead altogether. I hope I shall be put in my grave as soon as I'm dead; I don't want to walk about so.' Here we always differed! I thought the degradation of nature she feared was a consequence of poverty, and that she should give her attention to earning money. Sometimes she admitted this, but could find no means of earning money. At others she seemed afraid of letting her thoughts dwell on the subject, saying it brought on the worst palsy of all. Indeed, in her position, nothing less than entire constant absorption in petty money matters could have scraped together a provision.

Of course artists and authors stood high with Charlotte, and the best thing after their works would have been their company. She used very inconsistently to rail at money and money-getting, and then wish she was able to visit all the large towns in Europe, see all the sights, and know all the celebrities. This was her notion of literary fame—a passport to the society of clever people. [Mrs Gaskell's omission.] When she had become acquainted with the people and ways at Brussels her life became monotonous, and she fell into the same hopeless state as at Miss Wooler's, though in a less degree. I wrote to her, urging her to go home or elsewhere; she had got what she wanted (French), and there was at least novelty in a new place, if no improvement. That if she sank into deeper gloom she would not have energy to go, and she was too far from home for her friends to hear of her condition and order her home as they had done from Miss Wooler's. She wrote that I had done her a great service, that she would certainly follow my advice, and was much obliged to me. I have often wondered at this letter. Though she patiently tolerated advice she could always quietly put it aside, and do as she thought fit. More than once afterwards she mentioned the 'service' I had done her. She sent me £10 to New Zealand, on hearing some exaggerated accounts of my circumstances, and told me she hoped it would come in seasonably; it was a debt she owed me 'for the service I had done her.' I should think £10 was a quarter of her income. The 'service' was mentioned as an apology, but kindness was the real motive.[2]

7. [p. 434]. [I was anxious to know from her friend 'Mary' if, in the letters which Charlotte wrote to her, she had ever spoken with much pleasure of the fame which she had earned. To this and some similar inquiries Mary answers—]

She thought literary fame a better introduction than any other, and this was what she wanted it for. When at last she got it she lamented that it was of no use. 'Her solitary life had disqualified her for society. She had become unready, nervous, excitable, and either incapable of speech or talked vapidly.' She wrote me this concerning her late visits to London. Her fame, when it came, seemed to make no difference to her. She was just as solitary, and her life as deficient in interest, as before. 'For swarms of people I don't care,' she wrote; and then implied that she had had glimpses of a pleasanter life, but she had come back to her work at home. She never criticised her books to me, further than to express utter weariness of them, and the labour they had given her.

---

[2] Cf CB to EN, 13 October 1843 (WS no. 165) for the 'service', and Mary's letter of July 1848 (no. 16) for the use made of the £10.

APPENDIX C

Martha Taylor to Ellen Nussey, 17 May 1832

Text from WS no. 22

Roe Head, May 17th, 1832.

Dear Miss Nussey,

I asked Miss Wooler if she would allow me to sleep with you next half year if you came to school and she said certainly and she said she hoped I should profit by your advice. Miss Susan Ledgard was asked to return home with us at the beginning of the holidays but she preferred going home first and coming to see us at haytime when I hope we shall have the pleasure of seeing you. When Miss Hall is returned from Lincolnshire she is going to stay with my sister and they are going to come to see me at school. It is not quite settled whether sister will come to take drawing lessons next half year or not. Miss Allison, Miss Hannah Haigh and I are going to the Vicarage next Saturday where I think we shall enjoy ourselves very much. I asked mother if Miss Maria Brooke might come to our house in the holidays and she said she would be very glad to see her any time. I wonder how we shall go on next half year without you and Miss Brontë. I think the schoolroom will look strange without Miss Brontë at the head of the class. Have

you heard that Miss Allison's assumed name at the marriage
is to be Lady Georgiana Harcourt she is to be a Bride's
maid. I shall be very busy for I am to be a Clarke a Foot-
man and a gentleman. In the first place I am to run into the
dining room with the Bride cake; then I am to perform the
office of clerk; after which I am to be a gentleman; and
Miss Hall says she will be very angry if the gentlemen do
not frequently ask the ladies to take wine with them. I am
going to try for the neatness prize but I am afraid if you
come to school I shall not be able to obtain it. I think I
shall feel Miss Brontë's loss very much as she has always
been very kind to me. I must now conclude, and believe me
to remain yours very affectionately.

Martha Taylor.

APPENDIX D

The Identity of the Château de Koekelberg

The whereabouts of the 'Château de Koekelberg', by which name the Taylors and Brontës always spoke of the finishing school in Brussels which Mary and Martha Taylor attended in 1841-2, has hitherto been something of a mystery. Now, however, both its proprietors and its position have been identified.

Madame Goussaert, née Catherine Phelps, who conducted the school, was the wife of Norbert Goussaert, whose profession is variously given as 'rentier' and railway employé. Their son was born in 1836 in Koekelberg, that area of Berchem-Sainte-Agathe which became an independent commune in 1841. Norbert Goussaert is registered there in 1838; the son died in 1856 at his father's house, given at that date as 123 Chaussée de Jette, when his mother is named as 'directrice de pensionnat', as she still is in 1875 on her husband's death certificate. The address at that date was 154 Chaussée de Jette, doubtless because of street renumbering consequent upon the cutting of the Boulevard Leopold II. Madame Goussaert died as a State Pensioner in 1884, at the age of eighty-nine.[1]

---

[1] Information derived from the death certificates of Martha Taylor, Ennemont Eugène Goussaert, Norbert Goussaert, and Catherine Goussaert, and from the birth certificate of E. E. Goussaert, all in the office of the Commune de Koekelberg, Province de Brabant.

The site of her school may be found on a modern map of Brussels at the point where the Boulevard Leopold II crosses the railway line running northward from the Gare de l'ouest.

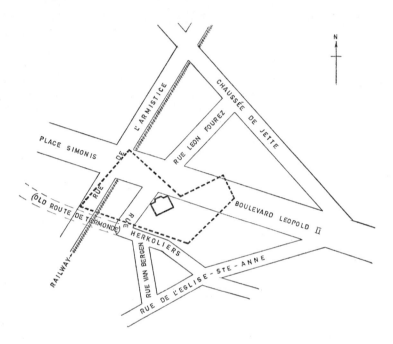

Here, in the survey of 1835 (approximately) was a plot of land owned by Desiré Vandenbogaerde, rentier, and held *in usufruct* by 'Goussart-Phelps, eigenar [proprietor], Koekelberg'. The property consisted of a house and garden, and the address is given as Chaussée de Jette, but with no number. Norbert Goussaert later became its owner, and sold the property in 1864 to an insurance company. It is described in the deed (drawn by the notary Vermuelen on 13 August) as 'maison de campagne, dénommée *Château de Koekelberg,* avec jardin, plantations et avenue, Chaussée de Jette', the *usufruct* being retained by Madame Goussaert. The new owners were expropriated in 1869 to make way for the Boulevard Leopold II. After a further transaction, what was left of the property was bought in 1878 (deed of 30 July)

by the Banque Nationale de Belgique. The house was demolished after 1888, and a school built on the site.[2]

The house is that painted by Henri Pauwels (1865-1959) whose picture, shown by Stepman in his book,[3] is reproduced in Plate 6. Pauwels signed his painting on the back, with the date 1887. The plot of land is that indicated in the map opposite. At the sale in 1888 some question arose about the Rue Van Bergen cutting across part of the property.[4]

This, then, is Mary Taylor's 'Château de Koekelberg'. Where did the name come from?

There is no connection, beyond the name, with the actual château, which had been demolished for a housing development in 1820.[5] Only the ruins of its tower remained in 1842; the present Rue Schmitz, leading to the Place des Etangs Noirs, was the old 'allée' of the château. Madame Goussaert probably chose the name as attractive to the international customers of her ladies' finishing school.

It has led to considerable confusion. Winifred Gérin asserts that the school was at the manor-farm of Karrevald (Gérin, p. 202). In two articles in *Le Folklore Brabançon* in September 1961 and 1962, Joseph de Mul gives another account full of discrepancies. In 1961 (p. 366) he says that the 'Pensionnat anglais' near the Chaussée de Jette was visited by Charlotte Brontë in 1881 (!), while in 1962 (p. 238) he writes that 'En 1843, Charlotte Brontë . . . alla au château de Koekelberg voir, sur son lit de mort, son amie Martha Taylor. On peut supposer que la romancière, arrivée aux Etangs noirs, emprunta l'actuelle rue Schmitz pour pénétrer dans le parc du château de Koekelberg.'

[2] Information supplied by the Land Registry Office, Brussels.

[3] Stepman, Charles et Verniers, Louis, *Koekelberg dans le cadre de la région nord-ouest de Bruxelles*. Bruxelles, 1966.

[4] Note in Pauwel's handwriting on the back of his painting reads :'Cette aquarelle date de 1887—L'immeuble a été vendu le 24 avril 1888—voir les registres du Conseil communal de Koekelberg où il était question de traverser la propriété par une fraction de la rue Van Bergen'. (Information by courtesy of Mrs Stepman.)

[5] Arthur Cosyn, 'Le Faubourg de Koekelberg', *Bulletin du Touring Club de Belgique*, 1921.

Both dates are wrong, for Martha Taylor died in October 1842, at Madame Goussaert's 'Pensionnat des dames anglaises' (as it is called in her death certificate) near the Chaussée de Jette, which still bore the name 'Château de Koekelberg' as late as 1864. The 'parc du château de Koekelberg' is nothing to do with it.[6]

---

[6] The protracted search for this material in Brussels was undertaken for me by Miss Andrée Art and Mr I. Prins, both of the Library of the Université Libre de Bruxelles, to whom I am very grateful.

APPENDIX E

The 'Pop Visit' to London: Charlotte's Letter of 4 September 1848

This, describing what Mary (Letter 18) called the 'pop' visit to London, is the only surviving letter from Charlotte to Mary. Mary sent it in 1856 to Mrs Gaskell in answer to her appeal for material for her biography. The envelope in which it travelled is postmarked at Wellington for 19 and 23 January 1856, having been returned for extra postage. The Manchester postmark on arrival is 14 May 1856.

In October, Mrs Gaskell lent the letter to Smith Elder's reader, Mr W. S. Williams, saying that it was 'particularly interesting as being the *other side* of an account I had already received', obviously from George Smith himself (Gaskell, *Letters,* no. 314a).

In 1900, C. K. Shorter in his edition of Mrs Gaskell's *Life* gave in a footnote to her summarized account of this London visit what purported to be the full original text of this letter of Charlotte's. It is nothing of the kind, being both inaccurate and seriously incomplete. Shorter's mangled version has, unfortunately, remained the only one in print, and has misled biographers in several important respects, not the least in presenting them with Shorter's 'snowstorm' in place of the *thunderstorm* of Charlotte's own words. George Smith's version of the events of that July weekend was written long after the event (*Cornhill Magazine,* December 1900), and is less reliable in detail, obviously, than Charlotte's vivid narration.

The circumstances that led to the visit are these. *Jane Eyre,* by Currer Bell, was published by Smith Elder in October 1847; *Agnes Grey* and *Wuthering Heights* by Acton Bell and Ellis Bell were published by T. C. Newby in December 1847. Newby then published Acton Bell's *The Tenant of Wildfell Hall* in June 1848, and allowed it to be understood that all these novels, *The Tenant* included, were by the one writer only, *Jane Eyre*'s Currer Bell. Alarmed at these discrepancies, Charlotte's publishers wrote to her about the problem in a letter which she received at Haworth on Friday 7 July. She and Anne decided at once that only a personal interview would prove their separate identities. They went straight up to London, and stayed at the only place they knew of, the Chapter Coffee House in Paternoster Row, where the party had stayed on its way to Brussels in February 1842.

See Joan Stevens, 'Woozles in Brontëland', *Studies in Bibliography,* 1971, for full details of Shorter's omissions and alterations.

Charlotte Brontë to Mary Taylor, 4 September 1848. Text from MS., Manchester University Library. Printed as no. 390 by WS in a grossly defective version.

Haworth.   Septr. 4th 1848.

Dear Polly

I write to you a great many more letters than you write to me—though whether they all reach you or not, Heaven knows. I daresay you will not be without a certain desire to know how our affairs get on—I will give you therefore a notion as briefly as may be.

"Acton Bell" has published another book—it is in 3 vols but I do not like it quite as well as "Agnes Grey" the subject not being such as the author had pleasure in handling —it has been praised by some reviewers and blamed by

others—as yet only £25 have been realised for the copyright
—and as "Acton Bell's" publisher is a shuffling scamp—I
expect no more.

About 2 months since, I had a letter from my publishers,
Smith and Elder—saying that "Jane Eyre" had had a great
run in America—and that a publisher there had consequently bid high for the first sheets of the next work by
"Currer Bell" which they had promised to let him have.

Presently after came a second missive from Smith and
Elder—all in alarm, suspicion and wrath—their American
correspondent had written to them complaining that the
first sheets of a new work by "Currer Bell" had been already
received and not by their house but by a rival publisher—
and asking the meaning of such false play—it inclosed an
extract from Mr Newby (A and E. Bell's publisher) affirm-
ing that to the best of his belief " "Jane Eyre" "Wuthering
Heights"—Agnes Grey"—and the "Tenant of Wildfell Hall"
(the new work) were all the production of one writer"

This was a lie, as Newby had been told repeatedly that
they were the productions of 3 different authors—but the
fact was he wanted to make a dishonest move in the game—
to make the Public and "the Trade" believe that he had got
hold of "Currer Bell" and thus cheat Smith and Elder by
securing the American publishers' bid.

The upshot of it was that on the very day I received
Smith and Elder's letter—Anne and I packed up a small
box, sent it down to Keighley—set out ourselves after tea—
walked through a thunderstorm to the Station, got to Leeds
and whirled up by the Night train to London—with the view
of proving our separate identity to Smith and Elder and
confronting Newby with his lie—

We arrived at the Chapter Coffee House—(our old place
Polly—we did not well know where else to go) about eight
o'clock in the morning—We washed ourselves—had some
breakfast—sat a few minutes and then set of [sic] in queer,
inward excitement, to 65. Cornhill. Neither Mr. Smith nor
Mr. Williams knew we were coming they had never seen us
—they did not know whether we were men or women—but
had always written to us as men.

We found 65—to be a large bookseller's shop in a street almost as bustling as the Strand—we went in—walked up to the counter—there were a great many young men and lads here and there—I said to the first I could accost—"May I see Mr. Smith—?" he hesitated, looked a little surprised—but went to fetch him—We sat down and waited awhile—looking a [sic] some books on the counter—publications of theirs well known to us—of many of which they had sent us copies as presents. At last somebody came up and said dubiously "Did you wish to see me, Madam?" "Is it Mr Smith?" I said looking up through my spectacles at a young, tall, gentlemanly man "It is". I then put his own letter into his hand directed to "Currer Bell". He looked at it—then at me—again—yet again. I laughed at his queer perplexity—A recognition took place—I gave my real name—"Miss Brontë—" We were both hurried from the shop into a little back room—ceiled with a great skylight and only large enough to hold 3 chairs and a desk—and there explanations were rapidly gone into—Mr. Newby being anathematized, I fear with undue vehemence. Smith hurried out and returned quickly with one whom he introduced as Mr Williams —a pale, mild, stooping man of fifty—very much like a faded Tom Dixon—Another recognition—a long, nervous shaking of hands—then followed talk—talk—talk—Mr. Williams being silent—Mr. Smith loquacious—

"Allow me to introduce you to my mother and sisters—How long do you stay in London? You must make the most of the time—to-night you must go to the Italian opera—you must see the Exhibition—Mr. Thackeray would be pleased to see you—If Mr. Lewes knew "Currer Bell" was in town —he would have to be shut up—I will ask them both to dinner at my house etc." I stopped his projects and discourse by a grave explanation—that though I should very much like to see Mr Lewes and still more Mr. Thackeray—we were as resolved as ever to preserve our incognito—We had only confessed ourselves to our publisher—in order to do away with the inconveniences that had arisen from our too well preserved mystery—to all the rest of the world we must be "gentlemen" as heretofore.

Williams understood me directly—Smith comprehended by slower degrees—he did not like the quiet plan—he would have liked some excitement, eclat etc.

He then urged us to meet a literary party incognito—he would introduce us a [sic] "country cousins" The desire to see some of the personages whose names he mentioned—kindled in me very strongly—but when I found in further examination that he could not venture to ask such men as Thackeray etc. at a short notice, without giving them a hint as to whom they were to meet, I declined even this—I felt it would have ended in our being made a show of—a thing I have ever resolved to avoid.

Then he said we must come and stay at his house—but we were not prepared for a long stay and declined this also—as we took our leave—he told us he should bring his sisters to call on us that evening—We returned to our Inn—and I paid for the excitement of the interview by a thundering head-ache and harrassing [sic] sickness—towards evening as I got no better and expected the Smiths to call I took a strong dose of sal volatile—it roused me a little—still I was in grievous bodily case when they were announced—they came in two elegant, young ladies in full dress—prepared for the Opera—Smith himself in evening costume white gloves etc a distinguished, handsome fellow enough—We had by no means understood that it was settled that we were to go to the Opera—and were not ready—Moreover we had no fine, elegant dresses either with us or in the world. However on brief rumination, I though [sic] it would be wise to make no objections—I put my headache in my pocket—we attired ourselves in the plain—high-made, country garments we possessed—and went with them to their carriage—where we found Williams likewise in full dress. They must have thought us queer, quizzical looking beings—especially me with my spectacles—I smiled inwardly at the contrast which must have been apparent between me and Mr. Smith as I walked with him up the crimson carpeted staircase of the Opera House and stood amongst a brilliant throng at the box-door which was not yet open. Fine ladies and gentlemen glanced at us with a slight, graceful superciliousness quite

warranted by the circumstances—Still I felt pleasurably ex-
cited—in spite of head-ache sickness and conscious clownish-
ness, and I saw Anne was calm and gentle which she always
is—

The Performance was Rosini's [sic] opera of the "Barber
of Seville—" very brilliant though I fancy there are things
I should like better—We got home after one o'clock—We
had never been in bed the night before—had been in constant excitement for 24 hours—you may imagine we were
tired.

The next day—(Sunday) Mr. Williams came early to
take us to church—he was so quiet but so sincere in his
attentions—one could not but have a most friendly leaning
towards him—he has a nervous hesitation in speech and a
difficulty in finding appropriate language in which to express himself—which throws him into the background in
conversation—but I had been his correspondent—and therefore knew with what intelligence he could write—so that I
was not in danger of underrating him. In the afternoon—
Mr. Smith came in his carriage with his Mother—to take
us to his house to dine—I should mention by the way that
neither his mother nor his sisters knew who we were—and
their strange perplexity would have been ludicrous if one
had dared to laugh—To be brought down to a part of the
city into whose obscure, narrow streets they said they had
never penetrated before—to an old, dark strange-looking
Inn—to take up in their fine carriage a couple of odd-looking
country-women—to see their elegant, handsome son and
brother treating with scrupulous politeness these insignificant
spinsters must have puzzled them thoroughly Mr. Smith's
residence is at Bayswater, 6 miles from Cornhill—a very
fine place—the rooms—the drawing-room especially looked
splendid to us. There was no company—only his mother
his two grown up sisters—and his brother a lad of 12-13 and
a little sister—the youngest of the family—very like himself
—they are all dark-eyed—dark-haired and have clear and
pale faces—the Mother is a portly, handsome woman of her
age—and all the children more or less well-looking—one of
the daughters decidedly pretty—except that the expression

of her countenance—is not equal to the beauty of her features. We had a fine dinner—which neither Anne nor I had appetite to eat—and were glad when it was over—I always feel under awkward constraint at table. Dining-out would be a hideous bore to me.

Mr. Smith made himself very pleasant—he is a firm, intelligent man of business though so young—bent on getting on—and I think desirous to make his way by fair, honorable means—he is enterprising—but likewise cool and cautious. Mr. Smith is *practical* man—I wish Mr. Williams were more so—but he is altogether of the contemplative, theorizing order—Mr Williams lives too much in abstractions—

On Monday we went to the Exhibition of the Royal Academy—the National Gallery, dined again at Mr. Smith's —then went home with Mr Williams to tea—and saw his /comparatively/ humble but neat residence and his fine family of eight children—his wife was ill. A daughter of Leigh Hunts' [sic] was there—she sung some little Italian airs which she had picked up amongst the peasantry in Tuscany, in a manner that charmed me—For herself she was a rattling good-natured personage enough—

On Tuesday morning we left London—laden with books Mr. Smith had given us—and got safely home. A more jaded wretch than I looked when I returned, it would be difficult to conceive—I was thin when I went but was meagre indeed when I returned, my face looked grey and very old —with strange, deep lines plough [sic] in it—my eyes stared unnaturally—I was weak and yet restless. In a while however these bad effects of excitement went off and I regained my normal condition—We saw Newby but of him more another t[ime]

God bless you write CB

BIBLIOGRAPHY

Books, newspapers, periodicals and MSS. referred to in the editorial text.

ARNOLD, THOMAS. *The New Zealand Letters of Thomas Arnold the Younger*, ed. James Bertram. Auckland, 1966.

BREES, SAMUEL CHARLES. *Guide and Description of the Panorama of New Zealand*. London, [1849].

Brontë Society Transactions. Keighley.

BURKE, JOHN. *A Genealogical and Heraldic Dictionary of the Landed Gentry*. London, various dates.

CADMAN, HENRY ASHWELL. *Gomersal Past and Present*. Leeds, 1930.

[CARTER, CHARLES ROOKING] *Life and Recollections of a New Zealand Colonist* (*written by himself*). 3 vols. London, 1866?-75.

Chambers's Edinburgh Journal. Edinburgh.

CHRISTIAN, M. G. 'A Census of Brontë Manuscripts in the United States'. *Trollopian* 2-3, 1947-48.

CRADOCK, HENRY COUPER. *History of the Ancient Parish of Birstall*. London, 1933.

Dictionary of National Biography. London.

Dictionary of New Zealand Biography, ed. G. H. Scholefield. 2 vols. Wellington, 1940.

Dominion. Wellington.

Encyclopaedia of New Zealand, ed. A. H. McLintock. 3 vols. Wellington, 1966.

Examiner. London.

FOSTER, JOSEPH. *Alumni Oxonienses* (1500-1886). Oxford, 1891.

Fraser's Magazine. London.

GASKELL, ELIZABETH C. *The Life of Charlotte Brontë,* ed. C. K. Shorter. London, 1900. (Haworth Edition)

GASKELL, ELIZABETH C. *The Letters of Mrs Gaskell,* ed. J. A. V. Chapple and Arthur Pollard. Manchester, 1966.

GÉRIN, WINIFRED. *Charlotte Brontë: The Evolution of Genius.* Oxford, 1967.

Glasgow Argus. Glasgow.

GODLEY, CHARLOTTE. *Letters from Early New Zealand.* Christchurch, 1951.

GORHAM, GEORGE CORNELIUS. *A Genealogical Account of the Family of De Gorram.* Privately printed, 1837.

Greenwood Family Tree. MS. owned by Miss Daphne Greenwood.

HALLÉ, C. E. AND MARIE. *Life and Letters of Sir Charles Hallé.* London, 1896.

HASELDEN, R. B. 'Scientific aids for the Study of Manuscripts', Supplement to *Bibliographical Society Transactions,* No. 10, 1935.

HOPKINS, ANNETTE. *The Father of the Brontës.* Baltimore, 1958.

INGRAM, C. W. N. AND WHEATLEY, P. O. *New Zealand Shipwrecks, 1795-1960.* 3rd ed. Wellington, 1961.

IRVINE-SMITH, F. L. *The Streets of My City.* Wellington, 1948.

LOCK, JOHN, AND DIXON, CANON W. T. *A Man of Sorrow: The Life, Letters and Times of the Rev. Patrick Brontë, 1777-1861.* London, 1965.

Manchester Examiner and Times. Manchester.

MILLER, JOHN. *Early Victorian New Zealand.* London, 1958.

New Zealand Journal. London.

New Zealand Free Lance. Wellington.

New Zealand Spectator and Cooks Straits Guardian. Wellington.

New-Zealander. Auckland.

NUSSEY, JOHN T. M. 'Walker and Nussey—Royal Apothecaries 1784-1860', *Medical History,* London, vol. XIV, No. 1, January 1970.

NUSSEY, JOHN T. M. 'Rydings—Home of Ellen Nussey', *Brontë Society Transactions,* vol. 15, No. 3, 1968.

NUSSEY, JOHN T. M. 'Notes on the background of three incidents in the lives of the Brontës', *Brontë Society Transactions*, vol. 15, No. 4, 1969.

NUSSEY, JOHN T. M. Nussey Family Tree, MS.

OLIVER, RICHARD ALDWORTH. Letterbook of H.M. Sloop 'Fly', 1847-51. MS., Alexander Turnbull Library, Wellington.

OLIVER, W. H. *The Story of New Zealand*. London, 1960.

PALMER, C. J. *The Perlustration of Great Yarmouth, with Gorleston and Southtown*. 3 vols. Great Yarmouth, 1872-75.

PEEL, FRANK. *Spen Valley Past and Present*. Heckmondwike, 1893.

PIGOT, JAMES. *Pigot and Co's Royal National and Commercial Directory . . . Counties of York . . .* Manchester, 1841.

SHAEN, M. J. (ed) *Memorials of Two Sisters, Susanna and Catherine Winkworth*. London, 1908.

SHEARD, MICHAEL. *Records of the Parish of Batley*. Worksop, 1894.

SHORTER, C. K. *The Brontës: Life and Letters*. 2 vols. London, 1908.

SHORTER, C. K. *Charlotte Brontë and Her Circle*. London, 1896.

SMITH, GEORGE M. 'Charlotte Brontë', *Cornhill Magazine*, n.s. vol. lx, December 1900.

STEAD, J. J. 'The *Shirley* Country', *Brontë Society Transactions*, vol. 1, No. 7, July 1897.

STEPMAN, CHARLES, ET VERNIERS, LOUIS. *Koekelberg dans le cadre de la région nord-ouest de Bruxelles*. Bruxelles, 1966.

STEVENS, JOAN. 'Sidelights on *Shirley*' and 'Her Own Landmarks: Mary Taylor's shop in New Zealand', *Brontë Society Transactions*, vol. 15, No. 4, 1969.

STEVENS, JOAN. 'Brother Fred and the Two Cultures: New Zealand's First Librarian', *New Zealand Libraries*, vol. 31 No. 5, October 1968.

STEVENS, JOAN. 'Woozles in Brontëland', *Studies in Bibliography*, vol. XXIV, 1971.

STEVENS, JOAN. ' A Note on Mossmans', *Brontë Society Transactions*, 1971.

STRAUBEL, C. R. (ed) *The Whaling Journal of Capt. W. B. Rhodes.* Christchurch, [1954].

TAYLOR, MARY. *The First Duty of Women.* Reprinted from the *Victoria Magazine,* London, 1865-70. London, 1870.

TAYLOR, MARY. *Miss Miles, or, A Tale of Yorkshire life 60 years ago.* London, 1890.

TAYLOR, MARY. (Contributor) *Swiss Notes by Five Ladies.* Leeds, 1875.

VALLANCE, CHARLES AUGUSTUS. MS. Journal, Levin Papers, Alexander Turnbull Library, Wellington.

WAKEFIELD, EDWARD JERNINGHAM. *Adventure in New Zealand.* London, 1845. 2nd edition, Wellington, 1908.

WARD, LOUIS E. *Early Wellington.* Wellington, [1929].

Wellington and Southern Province Almanac. Wellington, 1853.

Wellington Independent. Wellington.

WHITAKER, ROBERT SANDERSON. *Whitaker of Hesley Hall, Grayshott Hall, Pylewell Park and Palermo.* London, 1907.

WHITE, WILLIAM. *Directory of . . . Leeds.* Sheffield, 1843.

WHITE, WILLIAM. *History, Gazetteer and Directory of Norfolk.* Sheffield, 1845, 1854.

WHITE, WILLIAM. *History, Gazetteer and Directory of the West Riding of Yorkshire.* Sheffield, 1838.

WISE, THOMAS J., AND SYMINGTON, JOHN ALEXANDER (ed) *The Brontës: Their Lives Friendships and Correspondence.* 4 vols. Oxford, 1932. (The Shakespeare Head Brontë.)

WOODHOUSE, A. E. *George Rhodes of the Levels.* Auckland, 1937.

WROOT, HERBERT E. *The Persons and Places of the Brontë Novels.* London, 1965. Reprinted from *Brontë Society Transactions* vol. 111, 1906.

INDEX